Teaching Toward Freedom

Also by William Ayers

AS AUTHOR

A Kind and Just Parent: The Children of Juvenile Court

Fugitive Days: A Memoir

To Teach: The Journey of a Teacher

The Good Preschool Teacher: Six Teachers Reflect on Their Lives

On the Side of the Child: Summerhill Revisited

Teaching the Personal and the Political:
    Essays on Hope and Justice

Prairie Fire

To Become a Teacher: Making a Difference in Children's Lives

AS EDITOR

Teacher Lore: Learning from Our Own Experiences

A Light in Dark Times: Maxine Greene and the
    Unfinished Conversation

Teaching for Social Justice: A Democracy and Education Reader

A Simple Justice: The Challenge of Small Schools

Zero Tolerance: Resisting the Drive for Punishment in Our Schools
    —A Handbook for Parents, Students, Educators, and Citizens

City Kids/City Teachers: Reports from the Front Row

Teaching Toward Freedom

MORAL COMMITMENT

AND ETHICAL

ACTION IN THE CLASSROOM

William Ayers

BEACON
150
Beacon Press, Boston

BEACON PRESS
25 Beacon Street
Boston, Massachusetts 02108-2892
www.beacon.org

Beacon Press books are published under the auspices of the
UNITARIAN UNIVERSALIST ASSOCIATION of CONGREGATIONS.

12 11 10 09   6 5 4 3 2

This book is printed on acid-free paper that meets the uncoated paper ANSI/NISO
specifications for permanence as revised in 1992.

Text design by Isaac Tobin
Composition by Wilsted and Taylor Publishing Services

Library of Congress Cataloging-in-Publication Data

Ayers, William, 1944–
Teaching toward freedom : moral commitment and ethical action in the classroom /
William Ayers.
   p. cm.
   ISBN 978-0-8070-3269-5 (pb : alk. paper)
   1. Teaching—Moral and ethical aspects—United States. 2. Teachers—United
States. I. Title.

   LB1775.2.A94 2004
   371.102—dc22

                                                             2004004645

The world only spins forward. . . . More Life.
The Great Work begins.

TONY KUSHNER
Angels in America

Contents

Introduction

Moral and ethical matters power and punctuate life in schools and in classrooms, from Monday to Friday, from morning till night. Looking for ways to animate the moral heart of teaching, I turn not so much to research or the social sciences, but again and again to imaginative literature. I am drawn to it, I think, in the spirit of Franz Kafka's excited image of literature as an "ax that breaks open the frozen sea inside us." Kafka reminds us that we need to be broken open now and then, to keep our minds from freezing, to keep our spirits from dying, to keep the possibility of freedom alive. In "Telescope, Well Bucket, Furnace: Poetry beyond the Classroom," an essay in the *Writer's Chronicle* (March/April 2003), the poet Jane Hirshfield evokes Kafka and others and then offers her own delightful image: "Great poetry is not a donkey carrying obedient sentiment in pretty forms, it is a bird of prey tearing open whatever needs to be opened." The current desiccated discourse on teaching and schooling needs urgently to be torn open, and sooner rather than later—bring on the artists! Release the birds of prey!

Hirshfield adds that "there is only one reason to read a poem, and that is to find your way to a larger life than would otherwise be yours to live." We find in imaginative literature of all kinds, as almost nowhere else, an affirmation of that larger life, of human freedom and complexity, of the seemingly infinite potential to be and to become practically anything—monster and saint, hero and villain, noble and savage, evil and good, free and entangled, often at the same time, in the same character, and in the same story. When exploring something as complex, idiosyncratic, dense, and intimate as teaching, literature might help us find our way to that larger life, a life beyond the arid precincts of program and policy.

Teachers can, of course, be the midwives of hope or the purveyors of determinism and despair. It all depends on context and choice. Teachers can teach toward freedom, and teachers can conversely represent and practice a kind of "unfreedom"—subjugation, repression, agents of dependence and subservience. In *Beloved*, for example, Toni Morrison's 1987 novel of slavery, freedom, and the complexities of a mother's love, Schoolteacher comes to the plantation Sweet Home with an efficient and scientific interest in the slaves living there. Schoolteacher is a disturbing and jarring character for anyone who thinks of teachers as naturally caring and compassionate people, because he embodies something quite different: cold brutality, abominable sadism, towering arrogance linked to profound ignorance. Perversely fascinated with the mechanics of control and management, Schoolteacher is a prop in the system of dehumanization, oppression, exploitation—we feel the devastating impact of his work on the human beings he objectifies and uses—and he is on the frontline, personally making life unbearable for the people at Sweet Home. The fictional Schoolteacher adds depth to our understanding of the possibility of wickedness and evil in the life of teaching. He shows us teaching as unfreedom, teaching linked to the perpetuation of slavery.

Grant Wiggins, a different kind of teacher at the center of Ernest J. Gaines's *A Lesson before Dying* (1993), is faced with a seemingly impossible task—his elderly aunt insists that he visit a despairing and tormented condemned prisoner and "teach him to be a man before he dies." What can Wiggins do? What chance does he have? He doesn't even want to be a teacher, and he knows that such a visit will be resisted because the sheriff wants most of all a compliant prisoner, not someone stirred up with new ideas. Without much hope and without any plan of action whatsoever, Wiggins, reluctant and pessimistic, drags himself to death row, and with that single gesture Wiggins sets off a series of surprising changes in himself as well as in the condemned man and all who witness their encounter. The fictional Grant Wiggins is as compelling and real as any portrait of a teacher transformed in an authentic encounter with a student and the world.

Finally, Howard Baskerville, a character in Amin Maalouf's *Samarkand* (1994), is a British schoolteacher in the city of Tabriz in Persia at the time of the first democratic revolution. When Baskerville is observed weeping in the marketplace, he says: "Crying is not a recipe for anything. Nor is it a skill. It is simply a naked, naive and pathetic gesture." But, he goes on, crying is nonetheless essential—for when the people saw him weep they figured that he "had thrown off the sovereign indifference of a foreigner," and that they could come to Baskerville "to tell me confidentially that crying serves no purpose and that Persia does not need any extra mourners and that the best I could do would be to provide the children of Tabriz with an adequate education." "If they had not seen me crying," Baskerville concludes, "they would never have let me tell pupils that this Shah was rotten and that the religious chiefs of Tabriz were hardly any better." Howard Baskerville opens a window onto the complexity of teaching children who are not our own.

These teachers show us that teaching comes to life in context, and that pedagogy and technique are not the wellsprings of moral choice for teachers. Teaching becomes ethical action, the practice of freedom, when it is guided by an unshakable commitment to working with particular human beings to reach the full measure of their humanity, a willingness to reach toward a future fit for all.

I was dismayed—though not entirely surprised—to read in the *New York Times* that U.S. publishers have all but abandoned translating books from abroad ("America Yawns at Foreign Fiction," by Stephen Kinzer, July 26, 2003). According to a vice president at Harcourt: "A lot of foreign literature doesn't work in the American context because it's less action-oriented than what we're used to, more philosophical and reflective." And the executive editor at Hyperion Books added: "We have always been sort of monosyllabic in terms of languages, and that extends into ignorance or wariness of other cultures.... And the hard fact is that given the reality of the world, we simply don't have to be concerned about Laos, but people there might well want to be or have to be concerned about America."

I experienced a powerful synergy, absorbing these comments on foreign literature while simultaneously devouring, one after the other, *Balzac and the Little Chinese Seamstress* (2001), a novel by Dai Sijie, and the memoir *Reading Lolita in Tehran* (2003) by Azar Nafisi. The first is a work of the imagination set in the early 1970s during the Cultural Revolution in China, the second, a self-report from a professor teaching banned books in the fundamentalist-controlled Republic of Iran. In each there is evidence of the power of literature, the energy of art to change people's lives. In each there are tiny and surprising acts of resistance to authoritarianism and repression as the consciousness of characters expands in an encounter with forbidden fiction. In each, inspiration, affirmation, uplift.

There was something slightly off in my experience of these texts, however, something that felt not quite right. The unease came, I think, in how simple it was for me—an American, privileged in a thousand ways, neither subject to forced labor nor to imposed religious strictures—to read and enjoy them, undisturbed. I could climb the treacherous mountain path or slip silently into the clandestine meeting place from the comfort of my reading chair, and on a full stomach with a good night's sleep. It cost me nothing, I risked nothing. And so the question remains: What disruptive, humanizing lessons from reading might awaken us, might propel us off into new, important directions?

In the *New York Times* article cited above, Cliff Becker, literature director at the National Endowment for the Arts, called the turn away from world literature "a national crisis": "I am a citizen of the most powerful country the world has known, a country that asks me to be part of its decision-making process on a whole range of things. If I'm not able to experience other cultures, not even from a place that is as easy to reach as the printed page, that is outright dangerous." Becker is right, of course. Novels, poems, stories pose the large questions: What is meaning? What is our fate? How shall we live? While social science may presume to offer answers, art persistently poses questions. Art challenges and transports us; it offers an invitation to transformation and an opportunity to see things anew. Art can "make the familiar strange," and so it is not always sweet and pretty. As the poet Gwendolyn Brooks writes in the opening lines of "The Chicago Picasso": "Does man love Art? Man visits Art, but squirms. / Art hurts. Art urges voyages."

I try here to call on a wider world—often through the lenses of literature, art, and film—to urge voyages and to find my way into the truth of life in classrooms. I will summon up experience and argument to make a case for moral commitment, ethical action, and the possibility of choosing to teach toward freedom. Let me note at the outset that freedom, if it means anything at all, points to the possibility of looking through your own eyes, of thinking, of locating yourself, and, importantly, of naming the barriers to your humanity, and then joining with others to move against those obstacles. Freedom is not simply a gift—something inert, offered, received, accepted—but stands always as a challenge to "unfreedom," the active negation of a negative. Nor is freedom the same as complete autonomy—I cannot be anything I like—but it pushes us to act beyond easy resignation—"That's life.... What can I do?" Freedom, then, is an act, a verb, a force in motion; freedom must be chosen in order to be brought to life as authentic, trembling, and real.

The freedom we celebrate, the freedom we take for granted, came to life, after all, as freedom-in-action—the rebels at Lexington, the abolitionists and the runaway slaves, labor's struggle for the eight-hour day and women's fight for the vote, the civil rights movement, the modern women's movement, the gay and lesbian movements, and much, much more. The accomplishments and successes of these movements established new norms; looking back we can miss the uncertainty, the risk, the courage embodied in each of them. Each is an example of people defining their needs and their desires against the status quo. Each involved action, determined opposition, and an unpredictable future, each disturbed the peace, broke the law, and, yes, finally changed the course of history. Each began in a settled and a given world, and each reached toward something new.

The Chinese ideogram for "person" depicts a figure grounded in the earth and stretching toward heaven. What is she reaching for? What dream is she pursuing? Why so seemingly becalmed on one end, yet so relentlessly restless on the other? The character suggests the destiny of every human being: to be fated, but also to be free; to be both free and fated. Each of us is planted in the mud and the muck of daily existence, thrust into a world not of our choosing, and tethered then to hard-rock reality; each of us is also endowed with a mind able to reflect on that reality, to choose who to be in light of the cold facts and the merely given. We each have a spirit capable of joining that mind and soaring overhead, poised to transgress boundaries, destroy obstacles, and transform ourselves and our world.

Teachers live this tension with intense urgency—we meet our students as we are and as they are, right here and right now, finite but incomplete; we enlarge and expand in order to engage their minds and fire their hearts, to provoke their imaginations and our own. We jump into our work headfirst, we toil in the common fields while we hold open the possibility of something more, something transcendent—enlightenment, perhaps, and liberation. Each morning, as we rise and venture toward a new day, and later, as we approach our classrooms, we might remind ourselves that a teacher's destination is always the same: that special spot between heaven and earth, that plain but spectacular space where we might once again try to teach toward freedom.

1. Between Heaven and Earth

WHAT IS TEACHING FOR?

The allure of teaching, that ineffable magic drawing me back to the classroom again and again, issues from an ideal that lies directly at its heart: Teaching, at its best, is an enterprise that helps human beings reach the full measure of their humanity. Simple enough to say, and yet, in countless ways, excruciatingly difficult to achieve, and so it is worth restating and underlining at the outset: Education, no matter where or when it takes place, enables teachers and students alike to become more powerfully and self-consciously alive; it embraces as principle and overarching purpose the aspiration of people to become more fully human; it impels us toward further knowledge, enlightenment, and human community, toward liberation. And at the center of the whole humanistic adventure are students and teachers in their endless variety: energetic and turbulent, struggling, stretching, reaching; coming together in classrooms and community centers, workplaces, houses of worship, parks, museums, and homes. They gather in the name of education, assemble in the hope of becoming better, smarter, stronger, and more capable of rethinking and reconstructing their worlds; they come together to claim themselves as subjects—lively, awake, and on the move—in the face of blockades and obstacles and objectification. In the cosmology of the Brazilian educationalist Paulo Freire, this priceless ideal is an expression of every person's true vocation—*the task of humanization.*

Simple enough to say, as I noted, but bristling with tension and contradiction. For identifying humanization as a goal immediately suggests its opposite: dehumanization as both possibility and practice. Although education ignites initiative and courage, we know that some schooling is in fact the practice of obedience and conformity; if education stands in one instance for freedom and breaking through arbitrary and imposed barriers, we can point to other cases where it parades as a specific kind of repressive training, structured as steel bars and barbed wire. We are drawn inexorably into conflict.

Think of the teacher who extends the hand of possibility. Whoever you are, wherever you've been, whatever you've done, this teacher invites transformation—there is still something more. This is the humanistic concept of teaching: the voyage is under way, and we are pilgrims, not tourists. There is more to see and to hear. More to discover. More to repair and rebuild, more to create and construct. More to have and to do, more to be. The humanistic teacher's fundamental message, then, is this: You can change your life and you must; you can transform your world, if you will. The great work begins.

In Phillip Noyce's 2002 film *Rabbit-Proof Fence,* we see exactly the opposite—we are brought face to face with a vivid and harrowing documentary-like portrait of schooling as dehumanization. In the early twentieth century the Australian government established schools for aboriginal youngsters with the explicit "beneficent" mission of "civilizing the beasts." Destroying their identities, beating culture, knowledge, language, and memory out of the skins of native kids, emptying them completely in order to fill them up with the better stuff, breathing "whiteness" into them—all of this was "for their own good." It was a "lofty goal," the aim to "uplift the savages." Reactionaries would have destroyed them all, and it fell to the good liberals to create institutions geared to shaping native kids to fit the mold of proper white society, and yet, at the end of the day, able to participate only at the lowest rung of the economic ladder. "We're here to help," explained the government official in charge. "To encourage you in this new world." The fact that aboriginal families and children resisted these efforts—Noyce's film tracks two kidnapped sisters who escape from the school and trek thousands of miles across an unforgiving landscape toward home—was, to the settler mentality, further proof of the ignorance and backwardness of the "little people."

In *The Magdalene Sisters,* a film by Peter Mullan also released in 2002, we see a further example of dehumanization and degradation exhibited as education. Based on the life stories of several young Irish women sent to an asylum because they are deemed wayward—one a victim of rape, another flamboyantly flirtatious—the girls face a strict regimen of discipline-and-punish. The mission of the nuns who run the asylum is straightforward: to beat the sexuality out of headstrong, ungovernable girls—for their own good, of course, always for their own good. As in *Rabbit-Proof Fence* we experience the denial of thought, of expression, and of choice, the denial of the right to question and to decide for oneself, to make up one's own mind—the repudiation of the essential humanity of students. In each film we witness the horrifying process of human subjects being treated like inanimate objects. When humanity asserts itself, as it must, it is fitfully, painfully, and always as resistance.

These are important reminders that training can be in the service of oppression, that schooling can be the practice of dehumanization, "unfreedom." Still, for those who might see these depictions as exotic and foreign—one from Ireland, the other, Australia—somehow distant and unreal to our lived experience, we might do well to remember the forced sterilization of poor women in our own country, or the century-long Indian Boarding School experience in the United States—school as colonial outpost. Jeff Spitz's brilliant documentary film, *The Return of Navajo Boy* (2000), is the harrowing story of an American family mythologized in film and photograph—Happy Cly, matriarch of the Cly clan of Monument Valley, was called "the most photographed woman in America" by *Life* magazine, chiefly because of a picture of her at her loom, with towering cliffs in the background. Spitz uncovers the story of John Wayne Cly, taken by missionaries at age two while his siblings were away at boarding school and lost from his loved ones for decades. This is the story of a family shattered by the structured disregard of their lives and their hopes for themselves—through boarding schools, sterilization, land theft, unsafe work conditions, prisons, conscription, and more—and only reunited years later by a series of unimaginable coincidences and surprising events.

Francine Prose's 2003 novel *After* brings the problem of school as dehumanization even closer. She focuses on the fallout at a high school in western Massachusetts following a tragic school shooting fifty miles away. The newly hired "grief and crisis counselor," Dr. Henry Willner, is charged with helping the school "get back on track," and to "work in the trenches with high school kids in crisis." The teenage narrator points out, in his characteristically ironic sneer, that the shooting happened elsewhere, and that the school wasn't particularly off-track as far as he could see. This is commonplace stuff, the all-pervasive "trenches" metaphor, the easy assumptions of well-intentioned managers and bureaucrats, and especially the faux doctor himself.

Dr. Willner wraps himself in the posture of compassion and concern, and he speaks the "slanguage" of therapy and safety in a steady stream. At the assembly where he is introduced to the student body, he strings the clichés together, urging youngsters to share their feelings in the interest of "healing and recovery," "working through grief and fear," and "becoming better people." Funny thing, notes the narrator, there doesn't seem to be a lot of grief and fear; but, whatever. In this carefully constructed pop-psychology context, Dr. Willner suddenly drops a boot: "It is a virtual certainty that some of the privileges that we have all enjoyed may have to be taken away."

On this ominous note the downward spiral begins, first to the familiar terrain of hastily installed metal detectors, then to random drug tests and "zero tolerance," all leading to increasing suspensions and expulsions. New rules are instituted—they change every day—and punishments are severe. As more draconian measures inch inexorably forward, the school begins to resemble a prison in both tone and temperament. Parents are seduced and wooed, step by step, mesmerized by a barrage of frightening e-mails from Dr. Willner, or coerced and cowed into compliance through face-to-face confrontations in his office, where he plays good cop and bad cop simultaneously.

What is perhaps most disturbing is that Henry Willner, corrosive and malevolent as he is, is not quite the stranger we might wish him to be. Francine Prose told me that she had borrowed qualities from several teachers in her own child's high school, things that frightened or alarmed her, like the indiscriminate use of force and power without regard for its effects on human beings—a hallmark of authoritarianism. Willner was a composite, she said, a collage, and she had harvested his fictional assembly speeches verbatim from the actual pronouncements of U.S. Attorney General John Ashcroft, available in the daily newspaper. That's pretty close to home.

Dr. Willner may be a caricature or a type, then, but he is not from Australia, Ireland, or outer space. He is a vaguely familiar teacher in action—we note that there are Willners everywhere, and that there may even be a touch of Henry Willner in each of us. This, in the end, is what makes him both fascinating and useful—he is the fully realized authoritarian operative at work. Willner wears the mask of a teacher, but he shows us the face of the tyrant in full.

And why not? There are all kinds of ways to be a teacher, and the tyrant unleashed is a recognizable type. All tyrants—whether in a classroom down the hall or a workplace around the corner, whether ruling over a nation or a single sterile relationship—strike a certain domineering pose, talk a certain unyielding language. Totalitarian regimes and dictatorships, cults and sects, oligarchies and empires—the edges of authoritarianism in action are by now a commonplace: when the Supreme Ruler speaks, the masses are expected to listen, submissively. The leader makes a grand display of thinking and knowing, planning and choosing and acting—remember, it's not easy being the Great Helmsman—while the unfortunate (or alternately, the privileged) few anticipate being acted upon, and most just watch cautiously from the wings. Only the leader is invested with agency and power—no one dares share it—and only the head issues communiqués, which everyone hears but no one responds to. A custom in every authoritarian country I have ever traveled through—and this could be amusing were it not for the countless nauseating particulars and the bodies scattered underneath—is smiling photos of the Great One crowding the pages of the daily paper: opening an auto plant, inaugurating a bridge, greeting dignitaries, commenting on the future, addressing a conference. He is a whirlwind of energy and action—everyone else is freeze-framed: obedient, subservient, listening, and taking in. Thus the nature of the authoritarian.

The operative form of authoritarian communication is propaganda, always in the service of orthodoxy, always policing and top-down, never answerable. It is designed to manipulate and control, "to make lies sound truthful and murder respectable," as George Orwell said, to induce a dull nod of acquiescence, if not approval, rather than a critical or considered response. Propaganda is meant to be consumed, not engaged. When the lies are bold and transparent, the message becomes even more overbearing: "I have the power to speak falsely in front of you and you can't do a thing about it." The goal of authoritarianism is domination—people are to be compliant placeholders rather than free thinkers or active citizens.

Authoritarian education—schooling—is necessarily one-dimensional and unidirectional, always generated from on high and transmitted down the mountainside. The teacher is the Big Noise: thinking, acting, telling, directing, planning, choosing, controlling, managing, disciplining. The teacher knows the answers or will find them, knows the rules and will enforce them, knows the score and will settle it. The teacher has the whistle, the grade book, the desk, the chair, and the whip. Characteristically, the authoritarian teacher is never learning or searching, listening or asking or wondering. These things would subvert the carefully structured stance, undermine the precarious pose.

The student in an authoritarian setting is not expected to think much or discuss much, to contradict or to contest—she listens and takes in, she receives a world predigested and interpreted, meted out in discrete bits from others who, she is assured, always know better. She is obedient and compliant, isolated and lonely. In a sense she is simply tagging along, a tourist in her own life, her schooling running on a parallel track without regard for her input or her feelings, her hopes or experiences, her will or her vast choice-making capacity. Reduced to a thing, she becomes an object for endless manipulation— nothing about her seems to have any value in or for itself. She is a tape recorder, her mind a single-track, finite tape, 60 or 180 minutes, it doesn't matter. She starts school with an empty cassette in her head. Teachers turn the recorder on or off as they please. When the tape is full, she is finished. Schooled. The abiding lessons she is being scripted to learn are about rule-following and conformity, hierarchy and her place in it, agency and her lack of it, power in opposition to her own freedom. She is entirely fated.

Charles Dickens pegged this stance perfectly in the opening lines of *Hard Times*, written in London 150 years ago, in 1854:

> "Now, what I want is, Facts. Teach these boys and girls nothing but Facts. Facts alone are wanted in life. Plant nothing else, and root out everything else. You can only form the minds of reasoning animals upon Facts: nothing else will ever be of any service to them. This is the principle on which I bring up my own children, and this is the principle on which I bring up these children. Stick to Facts, Sir!" . . .
>
> The speaker, and the schoolmaster . . . swept with their eyes the

inclined plane of little vessels then and there arranged in order, ready to have imperial gallons of facts poured into them until they were full to the brim.

Almost a half century ago, in Brazil, Paulo Freire wrote *Pedagogy of the Oppressed* (1970), evoking the image of big-bellied and lifeless piggy banks (the students) being earnestly filled up by the teacher's daily deposits: "In the banking concept of education, knowledge is a gift bestowed by those who consider themselves knowledgeable upon those whom they consider to know nothing.... The teacher presents himself to his students as their necessary opposite; by considering their ignorance absolute, he justifies his own existence."

Here is the classroom as slave galley—the teacher merely beats the drum.

Schools do not exist outside of history or culture, of course: they are, rather, at the heart of each—schools serve societies; societies shape schools. School is both mirror and window—it shows us what we value and what we ignore, what is precious and what is venal. Our schools belong to us, they tell us who we are and who we want to be. Authoritarian societies are served by authoritarian schools, just as free schools support free societies. This does not mean that authoritarian schools with their propagandistic curriculum, manipulative relationships, and harsh, coercive methods necessarily produce people who lack skills—both Nazi Germany and Soviet Russia turned out brilliant doctors and scientists. Nor does it mean that they are universally effective in turning out mindless followers—they produce their share of rebels and resisters. For all the horrible examples of herd-like behavior and mindless and immoral conformity we can point to, we also note the ever present dissidents—totalitarianism fails to totally demolish the collective spirit, the fierce human will to be free. Still, in authoritarian schools the entire system is twisted toward mystification and geared toward control. If you know that a given society is fascist—Germany in the 1930s, say—certain classroom character-istics are predictable. You assume the tone will be lordly, the pedagogy domineering, the curriculum manipulative, even be-fore you take a first step into school, and you will often enough be right. Conversely, if you visit a school and see these same qualities, you might confidently predict that the government is hierarchical and imperious, even if it wraps itself in high and noble phrases: the Fatherland, the People, Patriotism—even Freedom.

Social strengths—confidence, optimism, fellow feeling—as well as weaknesses—pessimism, fear, mindless conformity—are reflected in society's schools. Inequities are on display, as are common hopes and shared aspirations. This in part ex-plains why classrooms from South Africa to China to Chile to the United States have been central sites of struggle for what people believe could be a better world.

Education is always enacted within a social surround, a community or a society, and schooling always involves usher-ing the young into some social order or other, into an entire uni-verse. So as educators, we must keep our eyes open: What is the existing social order? How do we warrant, defend, or justify the world as it is? What do we oppose or resist? What alternatives are possible? Surely none of us wants to be a colonial teacher of the *Rabbit-Proof Fence* tradition, a repressive instructor in the mold of *The Magdalene Sisters* school of discipline. Who, then, do we want to be? What shall we do? What are we teaching *for*? Schools are set up to induct the young, and so, whatever else they do, they enact partial answers to humanity's enduring questions: What does it mean to be human? What is society for? What is the meaning of life and what is "the good life"? What can we hope for?

From the perspective of a humane or democratic society, the authoritarian approach is always backward, always wrong—it undermines the participatory spirit of democratic living, it disrupts community, it aims to destroy independent and criti-cal thought. A functioning, vital democracy requires, in the first place, participation, some tolerance and acceptance of difference, some independent thought, some spirit of mutuality—a sense that we are all in this boat together and that we had better start rowing. Democracy demands active, thinking human beings—we ordinary people, after all, are expected to make the big decisions that affect our lives—and in a democracy education is designed to empower and to enable that goal.

Teachers in an open, democratic society must learn to think freely and without fear, to have and to use minds of our own, to discover and to make sense for ourselves without any connect-the-dots formulas, without bowing or genuflecting to any authority, and without any absolute guarantees whatsoever. This is required of us if we hope to teach students who will continue to develop minds of *their* own.

Education is always *for* something and *against* something else. It is a startling idea initially, this notion that we must choose, that education is not and never can be neutral. But the longer I teach, the clearer it becomes: colonial schools like those in *Rabbit-Proof Fence* served as props in the superstructure of empire; they were *for* the conquest and subjugation of the aboriginal people, and they were *against* the native people's culture, self-determination, and resistance; asylums and schools like the one portrayed in *The Magdalene Sisters* were *for* the church hierarchy and steadfastly *against* any notion of women's independence or sexual self-determination. No teacher in those circumstances could be entirely impartial. And neither can we—our stance cannot be wholly disinterested. At the deepest, most fundamental level, education stands either for human freedom and liberation, for enlightenment, or it stands for subjugation in one of its seemingly endless forms, from conventional, benign domestication to brutal suppression, subservience, dependence, capitulation. We teachers might, then, at the outset, choose to embrace *as principle* the idea that teaching is for us a humanistic endeavor, that we will stand up for truth and knowledge, liberation and freedom, and against oppression. Truth may elude us, of course, may be found only partially, but our eyes are open, our minds are stretching. Freedom may fall short, may be achieved only contingently, but our path is clear. Our stance and our goal guide us—we do not want our teaching lives to make a mockery of our humanistic values. We enter the territory of hard choices.

The idea that we must choose our teaching is not difficult to see in the extreme: *Rabbit-Proof Fence* shows us the curriculum as propaganda; *The Magdalene Sisters* illustrates an instructional strategy that is all indoctrination. But perhaps it is harder to see in less extravagant contexts. In our teaching, in our educational projects, we might do well to foreground the questions and make them explicit: What am I teaching *for?* And what am I teaching *against?*

These are, of course, ethical questions, and teachers—while they may be guided by some universal code or abstract form— soon realize that classroom ethics is a down-to-earth, practical affair worked out on the ground by ordinary people. Universals can certainly help—Love Your Neighbor; Don't Lie; Practice What You Preach—because universal principles, as Susan Sontag noted in an essay in the *Nation* (May 5, 2003), "invite us to clean up our act... to turn away from compromise, cowardice, blindness." Principles might encourage us to look critically at the way things are, which is too often hypocritical, "deficient, inconsistent, inferior." Universals can act as our signposts, even though they cannot settle each and every particular as it emerges.

Nourishing a stronger moral imagination—How does the other person feel?—is also a good idea. But neither universal principle nor vivid imagination is sufficient to settle every possible issue for all time, for moral decision-making always involves fundamental choices in which no system or rule or guru can ever fully deliver the answer. Nothing and no one can be made into the court of last resort. Because we are free, our moral reasoning requires that we at least try to see the bigger picture, that we struggle toward wide-awakeness and always new awarenesses, and still our ethical decisions are made through a process that is lonely, often intuitive, filled with despair and, finally, courage.

The 2002 British film *Dirty Pretty Things* by Stephen Frears offers a compelling example of ethics-in-action. Two illegal immigrants, Okwe, a Nigerian man with a mysterious past, and Senay, a young Turkish woman fleeing the prison of her circumstances, try to live decent, purposeful lives while they negotiate the subterranean worlds of modern London. Like other poor immigrants, they do the dirty work for the privileged, and they remain in large part anonymous and invisible to their overlords. They carry with them the weight of dislocation, the scars of all that they have encountered and endured, and they carry, as well, the hope that their uprootedness, their exile, will bear some sweet fruit some day, perhaps in the lives of their children.

The story turns on an impossibly complex set of choices Okwe and Senay will each have to make, choices between painful alternatives without any guarantees—the law will be broken no matter what they do, people will be wounded one way or another, and everyone will be changed in some fundamental ways. This is not a Column A / Column B kind of ethics: Abortion...bad. Death penalty...good. Stealing... wrong. Rather it is ethical choice—resistant and absorptive, anguished, unsettling, turbulent, and restless—in the swirl and chaos of real life as people must actually live it. Their eyes are open, they must choose, but for them there will be no easy retreat to the comfortable dining room to enjoy the roast beef at the end of the day.

My friend Greg Michie, a junior high teacher, tells a complicated story of a moment in the life of an eighth grader named Julio, "lumbering, baby-faced, and—to use his understated self-description—'kinda chunky.'" Julio came to Michie one morning just as the bell rang, looking worried. "I need you to hold my bag for me," he said in a tight, hushed voice. "Just till the end of the day." Greg figured that the kid had brought a pager or a pack of cigarettes or a *Playboy*, some kind of "technically-against-the-rules-but-really-not-such-a-big-deal piece of contraband" to school by mistake, but he soon discovered that Julio had a pistol-size BB gun plus ammo in his bag. Why? He'd been at his uncle's in the country over the weekend, got back to Chicago late and asleep, awoke in the morning, threw on his clothes, and picked up his bag without a thought about the gun. When he realized that he'd made a terrible mistake, he came to Michie for help.

Greg knows the Uniform Discipline Code—a thicket of Acts of Misconduct ranging from "Loitering" and "Being Improperly Dressed" at the low end to "Arson," "Sex Violations," and, yes, "Concealment of a Firearm" at the extreme. Punishments ran from teacher conferences to in-school suspensions to expulsion and arrest. Julio's predicament warranted a minimum of a six-to-ten-day suspension and a maximum of expulsion from school and notification of the police. What to do?

Michie's resolution involved intense reflection, dialogue, and seizing the teachable moment with this student. He held Julio's bag for him, saw him safely home, and nothing more came of the incident. Still, Michie anguished for months about whether he had done the right thing by Julio and by the larger school community.

Choices are often difficult and ethics is a daunting text any way you look at it—the principles of right and wrong, a discipline dealing with good and evil, a branch of philosophy stretching back to antiquity, a manual for right living, and on and on.... Ethics intimidates.

Moreover, ethical arguments are not just abstract, high-minded, and dense, but to presume that one is on the right side of such an argument implies a rectitude that nobody can sustain and very few—myself included—even aspire to. It gestures, then, toward self-righteousness. Is my life so damned exemplary? Am I in any position to pronounce moralizing judgments, to strike an authoritative pose, to condescend and to scold? Am I really so good? . . . Ethics terrorizes.

Ethics edges as well toward the religious and the political, where it is hotly declaimed and jealously guarded. Sermons on right living are the purview of preachers and, increasingly, of politicians, often in the form of simplistic one-liners for easy consumption. We feel our eyes getting heavy, our brains being packed with cotton wool. . . . Ethics anesthetizes.

But teachers must somehow move through that cotton packing, confront the intimidation and overcome it if they are to resist successfully the reduction of teaching to the instrumental, the merely serviceable, which commands so much unquestioned attention. For teaching, at its most fundamental, profound, and primitive core, is indeed ethical work. Whether they know it or not, teachers are moral actors, and teaching always demands moral commitment and ethical action.

The words "moral" and "ethical" both point to principles of right and wrong, to standards of good and bad behavior. Some people stipulate one as having to do with rules and duty, the other as more embedded, pointing to normative choices in practice, but in everyday conversation the words are interchangeable. To the extent that I make a distinction it will be this: "moral" implies the personal, the question of reason and thought, reflection and commitment; "ethical" gestures toward action within some explicit community.

Moral decisions involve choosing between alternatives, all equally possible. Jean-Paul Sartre tells the story of a student who came to him for advice about a decision he was wrestling with—Should I, the student asks, stay at home to care for my aged and ill mother, or should I redeem the family honor in light of my collaborationist father by joining the Resistance to Nazi occupation? The student is on difficult ground here, for merely being a conventional young man will no longer do—he cannot simply feel that he is a good person; he must now choose to act for the good, whatever that might be. After listening carefully to the reasoning of his student, Sartre answers as follows: You must decide for yourself. The student, then, is fully and finally responsible for his decision, without the benefit of blaming or crediting someone else. His eyes are open, and he must choose. Something will be lost, and something else gained. This, of course, feels dreadful—nothing is as clear or clean or absolutely certain as he would like. Frustrated and in urgent pursuit of higher authority, the student angrily denounces Sartre and says that if the great philosopher won't help him, he'll go to a priest for advice. Very well, replies Sartre, and which priest will you choose? The choice belongs to the student; he can object and in-sist and curse his mentor and his predicament, but in the end he will make up his own mind, and with that choice he will dive into the wreckage with all the good and terrible consequences to follow. Choosing his priest is still choosing, even if it appears noncommittal and neutral.

One day, when I was having coffee with a second cousin of mine—a twenty-one-year-old college student—she awkwardly asked me if I thought it would be okay for her to move in with her boyfriend. I told her the story of Sartre and his student, and asked her why she had chosen me to ask such a question. Why was I her "priest"? Why not, say, her own mother? Or why not make the decision for herself?

A teacher, of course, can help students think through histor-ical context and social surround, can point to the larger uni-verse of possibilities, and can offer alternatives that might be unknown to the student. A teacher can help sort out the differ-ence between a fact and a choice. Still, at last one chooses and one lives with the consequences of that choice.

These are moral questions: What is right and wrong? What is good and bad? What should I do in this or that situation? What is my obligation to others? These questions can help us to organize our thinking as we ask questions of our students: What will you do in five years? What do you want to do or to be? What is your aim, and your destiny?

The moral questions that arise are different in kind from

factual questions. A factual question might be, Where is P.S. 87? Or, How many kids below the poverty line attend P.S. 87? Moral questions are different: Should the school board spend funds on security or on the arts? Or, Should the board invest in a program explicitly to benefit the poor children at P.S. 87? Those questions cannot be settled by simply referring to evidence. They require awareness, judgment, and choice. Similarly, in a class you might ask, Is Molly here? A different order of question is, What is Molly's experience, what does she think and what does she require? In whatever guise, the classroom is a site where moral questions live—whether brought to consciousness or not—thanks to the implicit and explicit concerns that propel people to gather there.

Humanization and dehumanization—these quarreling twins define the landscapes of learning, and they make animating the living, ethical heart of teaching hard, grinding, often contentious, and sometimes courageous, work. The twins clash and struggle, become impossibly entangled and difficult to separate. It is not as if two distinct paths are laid out clearly before us—the bright heavenly path set with palm fronds, and the dark devilish path of briars and brambles. It is not as if at the end of the road there are two neat packages to choose between, one decorated with ribbons and roses, the other marked with a skull and crossbones. If life were like this we would always and forever live on the side of the angels. There would be only simple scripts to follow.

But reality is not like this. The choices we make daily in classrooms are murkier, denser, more layered, and more difficult. The implications of our choices are not always clear, the long-term effects not only unknown to us, but often unknowable as well. We walk our wobbly pathways as best we can, with hope, certainly, but without guarantees. All the more reason to hold in our consciousness the dimensions of what is at stake: humanity's capacity, drive, and potential for forward motion, the propulsive possibility of enlightenment, the unending quest for human freedom. All the more reason to bring our moral commitments to the surface for examination and argument. All the more reason—as we make our twisty way—to state from the outset our overriding commitment to humanity.

How odd, then, that this dimension and the fundamental choices involved go so completely unacknowledged and unspoken in our schools, not to mention in the wider world. There is so much talk about skills, so little about liberation. There are in-school seminars on classroom management and discipline, staff development workshops on lesson planning, but nothing on strategies to teach toward freedom. Formal authority supplants moral authority, and rule following trumps ethical reflection. The linear, the instrumental, the serviceable are emphasized without thought or question. The moral and the ethical are ignored, obscured, and obfuscated, also without much thought.

In colleges of education it is the same story. Professors and graduate students are too often rewarded for pursuing programs of research on teaching comprised of equal parts received thinking, gossip, cliché, shabby but somehow "proven" methods, and borrowed logic, packaged and presented to dazzle the credulous with the shine of "real science." The discourse on teaching narrows as it is refracted through the lens of research. Teacher-education and credentialing programs often have students dipping into educational philosophy, educational psychology, and history of education, picking up a few courses on the methods of teaching, and finally bringing it all together in a semester of student teaching. This approach structures the separation of thought from action, and nowhere elevates the moral and the ethical to a central place. All of this ignores the humanizing mission of teaching and, again, diminishes the heart of teaching.

I would like to see all teacher-preparation and graduate programs offer a course of study grounded in the humanistic mission of the enterprise: Turning toward the Student as a Fellow Creature; Building a Republic of Many Voices and a Community with and for Students; Feeling the Weight of the World through Your Own Lifting Arms; Teaching toward Freedom. These are the underlying values I try to bring to my courses. These are the themes that shape the chapters of this book.

There is a message here, of course, about what is to be valued and why, just as the message in the existing standard curriculum tells us what is to be valued and why. I want teachers to be aware of the stakes, and aware as well that there is no simple technique or linear path that will take them to where they need to go, and then allow them to live out settled teaching lives, untroubled and finished. There is in fact no promised land in teaching; there is instead that aching, persistent tension between reality and possibility.

I want teachers to figure out what they are teaching *for*, and what they are teaching *against*. I want to teach against oppression and subjugation, for example, and against exploitation, unfairness, and unkindness, and I want others to join me in that commitment. I want to teach toward freedom, for enlightenment and awareness, wide awakeness, protection of the weak, cooperation, generosity, compassion, and love. I want my teaching to mean something worthwhile in the lives of my students and in the larger worlds that they will inhabit and create. I want it to mean something in mine.

I want teachers to commit to a path with a certain direction and rhythm: become a student of your students first, and then create a lively learning community through dialogue; love your neighbors; question everything; defend the downtrodden; challenge and nourish yourself and others; seek balance. I want teachers to have a wild and eclectic and dynamic list that they can refer to when they are feeling lost or lonely. Here is Walt Whitman, in one of his many propulsive prefaces to *Leaves of Grass*:

> This is what you shall do:
>
> Love the earth and sun and the animals, despise riches, give alms to everyone that asks, stand up for the stupid and crazy, devote your income and labor to others, hate tyrants, argue not con-

cerning God, have patience and indulgence toward the people, take off your hat to nothing known or unknown or to any man or number of men, go freely with powerful uneducated persons and with the young and with the mothers of families, re-examine all you have been told at school or church or in any book, dismiss whatever insults your own soul, and your very flesh shall be a great poem and have the richest fluency not only in its words but in the silent lines of its lips and face and between the lashes of your eyes and in every motion and joint of your body . . .

Not a bad start. This is a list we can laminate and carry along in our backpacks, a list to tape to the wall. Written to poets, it stands as advice to those teaching toward freedom, too.

In the academy, in the political arena, and in popular culture, teaching comes in a variety of packages, each somehow inadequate. In the scholarly literature, teachers are observed and interviewed, our behavior sometimes dissected, then measured and set against student outcomes—we are a problem or we are a vehicle for change, but we are, without a doubt, data. Teaching as science.

In political debate, teachers are depicted variously—as serious professionals worthy of the community's praise if not its bounty, or as underskilled and unmotivated placeholders grown lazy in the sinecure of government employment. We are conduits of official curriculum—the stuff of classrooms—or the purveyors of some probably wacky or wicked ideas of our own creation, and here we inhabit a whole field of contention. Some focus on our dispositions and habits of thinking, others question our expertise and our proficiency. All seem giddily poised to spring upon our bleeding bodies. Teaching as work.

In popular culture we are knaves or knights, gods and monsters. The enduring film image of the teacher—from *Blackboard Jungle* to *Stand and Deliver*—is the solitary educator-hero fighting valiantly to save the good juvenile delinquents from the sewers of their circumstances. Teaching as salvation and as drama.

And it is true: teaching is drama, it is work, it is both science and art. Still, none of these images holds much sustainable interest. None is wide enough nor deep enough, none vital enough to capture the reality of teaching. None goes directly to the heart of the experience—to the intellectual demand, to the ethical purpose or the moral meaning, to the larger spirit that can animate the entire enterprise. What these stereotypes lack, even the seemingly benign, is any sense of the soul of teaching. It is this territory—teaching as a relentlessly moral endeavor, teaching as ethical action, messy, grand, and tangled—that cries out urgently to be explored.

The philosopher Hannah Arendt, in her 1968 text *Between Past and Future: Eight Exercises in Political Thought*, argues:

> *Education is the point at which we decide whether we love the world enough to assume responsibility for it and by the same token save it from that ruin which, except for renewal, except for the coming of the new and the young, would be inevitable. And education, too, is where we decide whether we love our children enough not to expel them from our world and leave them to their own devices, nor to strike from their hands their chance of undertaking something new, something unforeseen by us, but to prepare them in advance for the task of renewing a common world.*

Arendt provides a useful frame for considering teaching's moral landscape. We can see that school is a natural site of hope and struggle—hope hovering around notions of a future, struggle busting out over everything about that future: the direction it should take, the shape it could assume, the meanings it might encompass. Who can participate? What do we want for the children? And for ourselves? What worlds might we dream into being? What tools, skills, and accumulated wisdom should we offer the young, the coming generation? What might they create for themselves? Each of these questions invites us to reflect, debate, consider, and make judgments from conflicting claims.

We raise questions, doubts, challenges about the aims and the content of education. We explore the question of what teaching is *for*, and we proceed into the ethical.

In the opening scene of Ethan and Joel Coen's 1990 film *Miller's Crossing*, Johnny Caspar is struggling to explain to the big crime boss, Leo, how he has been wronged by an associate mobster, Bernie Bernbaum. "I'm talkin' about friendship," Johnny says, and the camera lingers on the frothy saliva forming in the creases of his thin, menacing smile. "I'm talkin' about character," he continues, structuring and shaping his case. "I'm talkin' about—hell, Leo, I ain't embarrassed to use the word—I'm talkin' about ethics" (which Johnny pronounces EH-tics).

Johnny is, indeed, talking about ethics: "When I fix a fight," Johnny argues indignantly, "say I play a three to one favorite to throw a goddam fight. I got a right to expect the fight to go off at three to one." Then Bernie Bernbaum, whom Johnny calls the "scheeney shmata boy," the lying cheat, hears of the deal, manipulates the situation, and the "odds go straight to hell."

"It's gettin' so a businessman can't expect no return from a fixed fight," complains Johnny. "Now, if you can't trust a fix, what can you trust?" Without ethics, he concludes, "we're back into anarchy, right back in the jungle. . . . That's why ethics are important. It's what separates us from the animals, from beasts of burden, beasts of prey. Ethics!"

"Do you want to kill him?" asks Leo coolly.

"For starters," Johnny replies earnestly.

As it happens, I first saw *Miller's Crossing* while I was reading William Bennett's *The Book of Virtues*. Leo and Bennett were both "talkin' about ethics." Bennett's résumé is long—secretary of education, drug czar, head of the National Endowment for the Humanities—but his singular role has been chief cultural warrior of the hard Right and public scold on all things ethical. He has a big voice in the school-reform debates, and his program is simple: undo public schools in favor of a publicly funded, meritocratic private school system. His program for America's children boils down to something equally straightforward: choose the right parents. Reading Bennett on right thinking is like hearing Johnny Caspar discuss ethics—oddly unreal, a bit bizarre, and, finally, deeply disturbing.

The proclaimed virtues under consideration in *The Book of Virtues*—self-discipline, compassion, responsibility, friendship, work, courage, perseverance, honesty, loyalty, faith—take on a distinctly ideological cast in Bennett's embrace. Leaving aside what he chooses not to reflect upon—solidarity, say, or thoughtfulness, integrity, passion, generosity, curiosity, humor, social commitment—here is Bennett's perspective on work, for example. In ninety-four densely packed pages we endure several poems about ants, some Bible verses, "Wynken, Blynken, and Nod," "The Little Red Hen," "The Three Little Pigs," "The Shoemaker and the Elves," "How the Camel Got His Hump"—and on and on. They add up to an irritable sermon on the importance of doing as you're told, the rewards of acquiescence and compliance, and the necessity of hierarchy and staying at your post no matter what. Theodore Roosevelt writes "In Praise of the Strenuous Life," and Ralph Waldo Emerson praises "Great Men." Booker T. Washington describes his climb "Up from Slavery" and Bennett, without a hint of irony or conflict, introduces him as a "soul who is willing to work and work and work—to earn an education." From Shakespeare, Bennett selects this bit from *Henry V*: "So work the honeybees; / Creatures, that, by a rule in nature, teach / The act of order to a peopled kingdom."

Naturally, there is no Marx here, but neither do we find Herman Melville, B. Traven, or Charles Dickens. And there's no Studs Terkel, either, someone who might have relieved the righteous preaching and probed the complexities and contradictions of work, the violence it can contain, for example, the ways in which human effort can lead to the transformation of people and their world, or the ways in which labor can be sometimes liberating, sometimes enslaving. There is no reflection on the modern context, the changing nature of work, and the urgent issue of displacement and deepening disillusionment. Instead, we are grimly instructed on the natural state of things: kings rule, soldiers fight and pillage, masons build, and porters carry the heavy loads.

What William Bennett accomplishes is a kind of *McGuffey's Reader* for his own little Kingdom of Do's and Don'ts, all served up in simple stories for simple living—little virtues celebrated at the expense of great ones. Bennett calls this collection a "'how-to' book for moral literacy," and separates the "complexities and controversies" of a moral life from the "basics." He distinguishes *lessons in ethics*, which he favors, from *moral activity*, which he advises suspending until maturity. I have an opposite view: The world of moral thinking and ethical action is as natural to children as any other. They are growing up in a physical world, true, but it is inseparable from a cultural domain and a moral universe. Moral thought and virtuous action in school begin with being cared for and accepted—teachers should demonstrate a fundamental belief in the unique value of each human being, and a recognition of our shared predicament.

At BJ's Kids preschool, a New York City daycare center where I taught for many years with an innovative and courageous teacher named BJ Richards, the air was filled with the language of ethics: "Is that fair?"; "Be fair." On a visit to the local firehouse, five-year-old Caitlin asked our guide, Jimmy, when there would be a woman firefighter at the station, and he exploded in derisive laughter. Caitlin was incensed. "That isn't fair," she stammered. Back at school, with BJ's help she fired off a letter to the mayor of New York. Here is an exquisite case of moral reflection followed by ethical action.

Yet for Bennett, it is important that youngsters remain passive recipients rather than active co-constructors of values. This view leads to the claim that "these stories help anchor our children in their culture, its history and traditions." "Culture" is of course permanently settled in Bennett's mind; lacking any sense of unease or obligation to think or to question, to expand or to reach out or to move beyond. A credulous believer in a stable "uniculture," and a principal warrior on its behalf, Bennett has blinded himself to the vivid, dynamic, colliding, conflicting, and propulsive power of cultures as experienced and lived by human beings. The ethical world he would impose on others is inert, flat, untroubled, largely disembodied, and often unfair.

Meanwhile, William Bennett himself is a whirlwind of activity, leading an unprecedented attempt to crush a great progressive and democratic ideal, the idea of a free common public school available to all. This ideal, it has long been believed, would promote the general welfare, allow for a broader participatory pursuit of happiness, help people live in harmony and freedom, model meaningful moral reflection and ethical action with the young. But Bennett and his allies—politicians, bureaucrats, and an intellectual cadre that includes the researcher Chester Finn, the historian Diane Ravitch, and the writer Abigail Thernstrom—are not buying it. They have tried to engineer the illicit marriage of powerful ideological forces with specific, seemingly discrete policies that together point to the abandonment of the idea that every child and youth is entitled to a free and high-quality public education. While that idea has never been fully realized—indeed, for over a hundred years struggles have raged over who should be included in our sense of the public, what knowledge and experiences are of most value and how they should be accessed—the idea itself seemed secure because it was assumed to be held in common, and now that is in doubt.

The evidence of its abandonment is widespread and multilayered. The accelerating obsession with a single, simpleminded, centralized test that can do little more than rank students—at younger and younger ages—along a continuum of winners and losers cuts at the heart of a democratic education, assaults any notion of a deep and rich curriculum, and undermines teaching. The energy and resources sucked into the business of testing represent a demonstrable drain on commitments to put more qualified teachers in classrooms, to lower class and school size, to increase curriculum offerings and access to community learning resources, or to build more modern schools. The same simplistic standard is being pushed onto teaching: a "qualified teacher" can pass a simple test, period. The testing business cheats students, families, and teachers materially, deceives them educationally, and is a step backward for education.

Zero-tolerance policies, which have swept the country in the past decade, fueled in part by highly publicized school shootings and morphing quickly to embrace a host of issues beyond weapons, create the conditions for the exclusion from our schools of large numbers of youth, especially poor and working-class kids, students of color, the children of certain immigrant groups, the disabled and the marginal, the officially or traditionally despised. Criminal justice metaphors and practices are embraced, and the great humanizing mission of education is lost. These policies are a cultural and political attack on the idea of inclusive, democratic schooling. Classrooms become sterile and one-dimensional places devoid of teachable moments: Every misbehavior warrants a trip to the office, teacher judgment and wisdom are curtailed, administrators become adjuncts to the police, and schools become narrower, narrower, narrower, until they are nothing more than little training prisons.

Finally, the whole range of school change strategies driven by a market model threaten to undermine the structures and the principles of public education. The marketplace has rarely had a heart or a soul—it is not designed to make judgments of value or answer normative concerns. The market creates a class of winners and a much larger class of losers. Success in the market is realized in profit—great wealth is generated through the labor of others. The imposition of a market metaphor on a public enterprise such as schooling is infused with disingenuousness, beginning with the fact that no salable product is produced in schools, and therefore money to function must come from a public fund. The metaphor, then, is false and on its head: public money will still be required, of course, but private interests will dominate the resources and benefit or profit from them.

Everything good is not the simple result of individual virtue—there is also the matter of community ethics, of social ethics, the question of how we behave collectively, what our society assumes as normative and good. After all, most of us, most of the time, do as everyone else does—most Greeks act like Greeks, most Romans act like Romans, and when in Rome we tend to do as the Romans do. This ecology of ethics leads to the realization that individual ethical behavior is much more likely in a just society. Johnny Caspar is arguing for ethical behavior in an inhumane enterprise. Is he moral? During the time of slavery there were undoubtedly honest slave traders, loyal slave-catchers, and plantation owners who told the truth, paid their bills, and lived up to their promises, but in what sense were they acting ethically? In order to be a moral person then and there—it seems so obvious now—one would have had to work for abolition. Not many did, but we find some comfort today in telling ourselves that we would surely have been among the courageous and the righteous few. But is it true? How do we know? We know that a slave society undermines goodness every moment in a million different ways. And since we know that it is very nearly impossible for individuals to live virtuous lives in a slave state, it becomes essential to end slavery—or in these times, to work toward a more just world—as part of leading a moral life. A just society creates the conditions for more of us to act more often in a moral way. Are there any injustices here and now that we take for granted and for which the coming generations might indict or condemn us? And most important, what social and community standards would allow or invite more of us to do the right thing? Could these become reasonable or even compelling questions for teachers and students?

What is fundamentally missing in Bennett is a sense of

morality or moral literacy or virtue embedded in a stance, a set of relationships and commitments. We are instructed in a rationalist ethics at the expense of relational morality, deprived of an angle of regard that enlarges our view. Bennett is the stern father with the austere regulations: he rebukes, he scolds, he shows us the iron hand. His moral authority relies for its power on structure, a structure secured by fear and the absence of dissent. Bennett abstracts questions of good and bad from their social contexts, and he nowhere links moral stance to ethical conduct—especially his own. Moral clarity, certainty, dogma: these are best delivered from above, through a megaphone. Which brings us back to Johnny Caspar talking about ethics. The bully is whining, wheedling, hectoring, and threatening as required. He is comical, and, in the same gesture, menacing.

In one sense, though, we might follow Johnny Caspar's lead: Let's agree that we ain't afraid to use the word—hell, we're talkin' about ethics. But when the moral or the ethical is invoked—whether in education or in a meeting of mobsters—let's also be wise enough to proceed with caution. "Morality" describes an entire domain, a territory without stable borders. The realm of the moral and the ethical is peopled with good guys and bad guys, with heroes, conquerors, exploiters, madmen, and con men, all of whom have evoked elaborate descriptions of "morality" to justify their bloody efforts. Many have found morality a convenient hammer with which to beat their opponents into submission. In schools and classrooms, appeals to the moral have been used to crush initiative and erase the creative, the new, the different. It is simply untrustworthy and unreliable as a word referring to any single, immutable thing.

The greatest monsters in history created for themselves an entire moral universe that they could access as rationale and guide, and this makes moral reasoning all the more fraught and bewildering. Bucking the tide is not always or necessarily moral, although it can be, but neither is going along. Being brave might be moral, but it might as often be foolish or even immoral. How to know? We are cast back upon ourselves, as Sartre points out, making our way as best we can. We must take an honest look at the content of our choices, the truth of our situations, and ask whether or not we are taking the side of humanity. Are we opposing unnecessary suffering, undeserved pain? How do we know?

We might begin with the deeply humanistic idea that human beings are the measure of all things—every human life is, by the simple virtue of being human, equal in value to every other. We value our students, and we take their worthiness as an act of faith. Our broad ethical task is to make life more possible, more robust, more full and fulfilling, more livable for each. For us teachers, this begins with opening our eyes to the kaleidoscopic reality of the world, and embracing our students, taking their side as fellow human beings. This seemingly straightforward goal is not so simple in practice, for it operates within a world of conflicting claims, of dilemmas and contradictions, and, most important, because it is worked out by finite and flawed human beings, with all our attendant weirdnesses and weaknesses and limitations.

José Saramago sketches a harrowing moral landscape in *Blindness*, his dark allegory of a modern epidemic and the atrocities it unleashes. A man stopped at a red light in rush hour goes suddenly blind. Around him horns honk, commuters become impatient and then enraged, a little chaos takes hold as people try to sort out what has happened. Someone helps the man home and then steals his car.

By the next day it has become clear that an epidemic of "white blindness" is spreading, afflicting people at an accelerating pace. One after another, people open their eyes and feel as if they've plunged into a thick milky sea.

The authorities at first quarantine the ailing, locking them in an empty mental hospital. When the guards go blind, the prisoners are abandoned, but not before a group of blind men organize themselves into a predatory gang, steal the food rations of the others, and humiliate and rape all the women, young and old.

When it seems the worst is upon them, one and then another and another, just as suddenly, regain their eyesight. In jubilation, laughing and hugging one another, they ask, Why? Whatever happened? Why did we go blind? Why do we now see?

A woman responds: "I don't think we did go blind, I think we are blind, Blind but seeing, Blind people who can see, but do not see." She is reminding us that the opposite of moral isn't always immoral—it is more often merely indifferent. Ethical action on one hand and on the other cool detachment, negligence, apathy, inattentiveness, incuriousness, aloofness. Blindness. Were they really blind? And now, sighted once more, can they really see?

"Blind people who can see, but do not see"—the nightmare Saramago evokes is the modern predicament in full, without window dressing. Blind people who can see. But do not see. For teachers this trembling metaphor has special meaning, for we are in a position to shepherd the choices of others. We must open our eyes to the world as it is, and to the world as it could be, but is not yet. We must see, for we must choose.

What is teaching *for?* It surely serves us to remember the various systems of moral thought and law that have preceded us, alongside their gaps, failures, and inadequacies. We want to make choices on principle, but we also want to avoid the deadening effects of orthodoxy, to embrace moral commitments and at the same time maintain a critical mind. We want to *act*, but we *need* to doubt. This stance asks us to proceed with caution, with humility, with our eyes wide open in order to face a chaotic, dynamic, and perspectival world, with hope but without guarantees. We stand at a juncture, at the place between heaven and earth, struggling to stay grounded and fighting to remain hopeful, our eyes open to possibilities of freedom and pathways to truth.

2. Turning toward the Student
WHO IN THE WORLD AM I?

"We love our children," observed the celebrated war correspondent Martha Gellhorn in a 1967 article for *Ladies' Home Journal*. "We are famous for loving our children, and many foreigners believe that we love them unwisely and too well. We plan, work and dream for our children; we are tirelessly determined to give them the best of life." Gellhorn draws something of a caricature of the American middle class: confident and forward-charging, overprivileged and, yes, stunningly myopic. "Perhaps we are too busy," she continues, "loving our own children, to think of children 10,000 miles away, or to understand that distant, small, brown-skinned people, who do not look or live like us, love their children just as deeply, but with anguish now and heartbreak and fear."

Martha Gellhorn was writing about Vietnam at the time of the sharply escalating American war there, but she could as easily be speaking to us today. We love our children, of course, but what, for example, do we know of the children of Afghanistan or Iraq, Syria or Palestine, places upon which our government has turned a specifically terrifying eye? Can we see them as three-dimensional creatures, much like ourselves? And, knowing or not knowing, can we imagine what it might mean to love or care for those children, or at the very least, what a mother there might feel for her child? What do we know of the children of Puerto Rico, Colombia, Guatemala, Liberia, or the Philippines—all places under direct American economic or military power? For that matter, what do we know, or care to know, of the children of the South Side of Chicago or, if we are of the South Side, then of the North Side, or of the east side of Cleveland? What do we make of our balkanized condition? What do we really know about our neighbors or their children, about those whom the dazzling and insightful teacher Lisa Delpit has called "other people's children"?

I have argued that teaching is fraught from the start with issues of duty and responsibility, allegiance and engagement, consciousness, commitment, conscience, and conduct. Teaching ignites enduring questions and concerns: Who in the world am I? What does it mean to be human? What is good and fair and just? What kind of world do we live in, and is there anything in all that we survey that is in need of repair? What should we bequeath to the coming generation? What might we reasonably hope for? The conduct of teaching engages these kinds of first questions, sometimes explicitly, often implicitly.

Education cannot be neutral—it is always put to use *in favor* of something and *in opposition* to something else. It is urgent, then, that we teachers, especially, struggle to open our eyes, to shake off our blindness and work hard to see the world as clearly as we can through the fogs of mystification and alienation. Those teaching toward freedom must recognize the difficult, seemingly impossible choices to be made, choices that are often submerged or hidden, alternately paraded as destiny or fate, common sense or fact, but choices nonetheless. Awareness and choice—this is the territory of the ethical.

At the deepest, most profound level education is an enterprise dedicated to truth and enlightenment, liberation and freedom, or, conversely, bent inexorably toward dehumanization in one of its many forms, from conformity to oppression. Teaching can be an exalted calling or it can be a degraded practice, but it cannot be both at once. To fail to notice this, to be blind to the ethical dimensions ceaselessly at work, in no way mitigates or diminishes that truth—it simply puts the teacher on a more slippery footing in terms of what she will face and find, and finally what she might accomplish each day in the classroom.

A dialogue on the moral commitment to teach and ethical action in the classroom draws our attention to something more than rule following or convention, classroom management or lesson planning, something more than the linear and the merely serviceable, something more than skills or even dispositions of mind. It highlights the larger purposes and deepest dimensions, the difficulties and challenges, conflicts and contradictions alive at the base of teaching. It might also help us negotiate the hard realities we face, and point to both the risks and the rewards of the teaching life.

Each of us—each of you, each of your teachers, and each of your students—is born into a "going world," a dynamic site of action and interaction stretching back into deep history and forward toward infinity. Each of us encounters an historical flow, a social surround, a cultural web. And each of us—each of you, each of your students—faces the task of developing an identity within the turmoil of multiplicity, of inventing and reinventing a self in a complex tangle of relationships and conflicting realities, of finding an "I" against a hard backdrop of "it," of facticity and "thingification."

All students, from preschool through adult education, bring two powerful, propulsive, and expansive questions with them each day into every classroom. Although largely unstated and implicit, even unconscious, these questions are nonetheless essential. Who in the world am I, or who am I in the world? What in the world are my choices and my chances? These are simple questions on the surface, but they roil with hidden and surprising meanings, always yeasty, unpredictable, potentially volcanic. They are, in part, questions of identity-in-formation, and in part questions of geography: of boundaries and of limits, but also of aspirations and of possibilities. Enrolling in a literacy class at the community center or an English-language class at a local college, leaving home to attend a university, starting high school or kindergarten—these questions boom inside: Who in the world am I? What place is this? What will become of me here? What larger universe awaits me? What shall I make of what I've been made? What are my choices?

No teacher can ever answer these questions definitively, for there is too much going on—life is too vast, too complex. The wise teacher knows that the answers lie within the students' minds and hearts and hands. Still, she acknowledges that the questions exist, that they persevere. She looks for opportunities to prod the questions, to agitate and awaken, to pursue them across a range of boundaries, known as well as unknown.

Who in the world am I? Knowing that the question exists, that it abides, points to a compact between teacher and student, largely improvisational, often implied. Brought to light, made conscious and articulated, it sounds something like this: I see you as a full human being, worthy of my effort and attention; I will do my best on your behalf; I will work hard and take you seriously on every appropriate level. In turn, you must, by your own lights, capture your education for yourself: seize it, take hold of it, and grasp it in your own hands, in your own way, and in your own time.

Committed and aware teachers, wrestling to engage this agreement, must endeavor to accomplish two crucial tasks. One is to convince students, often against a background of having attended what we might call "obedience training school," that there is no such thing as receiving an education as a passive receptor or an inert vessel—in that direction lies nothing but subservience, indoctrination, and worse. All real education is and must always be self-education. The second task is to demonstrate to students, and to yourself, through daily effort and interaction, that they are valued, that their humanity is honored, and that their growth, enlightenment, and liberation are the paramount concern. We take the side of the student.

Louisa Cruz-Acosta, a second-grade teacher at the Muscota School in New York City, develops a curricular theme each year. The theme in her 2003–2004 classroom was "Making Space." The children were learning to make space in their lives and their minds and their hearts for one another, for their neighbors, for members of the larger community, for animals, and for different cultures and new ideas. One of the Latino kids referred fondly to "*this* America," meaning he knew more than one, and yet he embraced his new home, his classmates, as a unique "gathering of souls."

Louisa tries to create in her classroom an "island of decency," a safe harbor where the most fraught issues can be talked about respectfully, candidly, deeply. Louisa communicates a vital sense to each student: It matters that you are here. Stay awhile. Speak and listen. Come back tomorrow.

She posits rules for herself and others that can help to create these islands of decency: Listen. View everyone as an individual, not as a representative of a group. Respect silence. Learn to live with questions that have no easy answers. Ask first; speak later. Be conscious of the way you use the words "we" and "they" and "you."

What and who do we see as we look out at our students? A sea of undifferentiated faces? A set of IQs and test scores, a collection of deficits? Are there any options at hand? And how do we position ourselves? As master and commander, potentate or patriarch? Do we rule our domain from a particular symbolic space, a throne, say, or a massive oak desk or a lectern? What are the alternatives?

The fundamental message of the teacher—the graduate school lecturer, the high school biology teacher, the preschool teacher, and everyone in between—is this: You can change your life. The good teacher provides recognition, and holds out the possibility of growth and a change in direction, the possibility of a new and different outcome: Here's a sonnet, a formula, an equation, a way of seeing or figuring or imagining. Take hold of your life, engage the world, and you must change.

We notice that our students are endowed with active minds, restless bodies, dynamic hearts and spirits. They are on the go. And full of surprises. Each brings a unique set of experiences and capacities to class, and each is filled with his or her own hopes and aspirations. Do we know what they are? How can we find out?

We begin by standing *with*, not above, our students. We share their predicaments, and we do so in solidarity with them. We look beyond deficits to assets and capacities, strengths and abilities, something solid that we can build upon. We seek some common ground to pursue growth and development.

Just like us, each of our students contains some spit and snap, some fire. Can we see it? Can they? None of our students is fixed or motionless, none entirely quiet or still—and if they appear thus, it is an illusion—every one is churning and charging, packed with energy, a quality that physicists define as the potential for change. This is how we might see them: as unruly sparks of meaning-making energy on a voyage of discovery through life. They are poised to change. So are we.

Martha Gellhorn's observation that people "who do not look or live like us, love their children just as deeply, but with anguish now and heartbreak and fear" admonishes us to recognize that every human being, no matter who, has a complex set of circumstances that makes his or her life understandable and sensible, bearable or unbearable. Each is unique in their walking of this earth, each an entire universe, each somehow sacred. This recognition asks us to reject any action that treats other people like objects, anything that thingifies human beings. It demands that we embrace the humanity of every student, that we take their side. Further, it might inspire in us a sense of reverence or humility, and more than a little awe—humility because we are face to face with our own limits, our own smallness; awe because we are simultaneously in touch with the infinite.

The actor and teacher Anna Deavere Smith captures some of this humility and awe in a riveting series of theater pieces that she calls *On the Road: A Search for American Character,* in which she interviews people—often in situations of conflict and stress—and later performs in their character, using their own words. In a single performance in her one-woman show, she might be a Baptist preacher, a drug dealer, a Muslim minister, a Hassidic mother, and a rebbe. Whatever image or stereotype or categorical thinking one might bring to any of those characters is exploded in Smith's portrayals—each is more than we ever thought, deeper, fuller, more surprising than we imagined. Each has dimensions we didn't know existed. The experience is both humbling and exhilarating.

Smith transforms herself on stage with astonishing speed and effect, and her major vehicle is words, how they're chosen and constructed, how they work with us and on us to shape an identity. Smith says she tries to create a space where the person she's talking with experiences his "own authorship," her own "natural 'literature.'" She claims that everyone in time "will say something that is like poetry." Her interest, remember, is American character, and "the process of getting to that poetic moment is where 'character' lives."

Anna Deavere Smith's work is rooted in empathy—it depends on seeing and listening to people's stories, their poetry, their own meanings, the specific words they choose to present to the world. This is an essential lesson for teachers, for this kind of seeing and listening goes beyond the surface and the superficial, requiring both effort and consciousness. The intent is honest representation, the approach is generous regard, and the work itself is arduous. "To develop a voice," she says, "one must develop an ear. To complete an action, one must have a clear vision." She wonders: If a female actor has an inhibition about acting like a man, or a black actor portraying a white person, does this point to an inhibition about seeing a man, or hearing a white person? "Does the inability to empathize start with an inhibition," she asks, "or a reluctance to see? Do racism and prejudice instruct those inhibitions?" As teachers, what do we see when we look at our students? What instructs our imaginations or our inhibitions?

A distinct inhibition on our ability to hear or see others fully or fairly is the reduction of humanity into categories, a practice that characterizes society in all areas, a practice so widespread that we hardly notice. We live within our inflamed identities with such fierceness that we tend to obliterate complexity, nuance, and truth. "I'm a feminist," "I'm a philosopher," "I'm a teacher," "I'm an editor." Even if true, the words say too much, take up too much space and cast too large a shadow. The literary scholar Edward Said insisted that "no Muslim is just a Muslim, no Christian just a Christian, no Jew just a Jew." We are each a whole universe, sailing through space. And yet we find our visions limited, our inhibitions schooled. I remember seeing a cartoon around Mother's Day in which a bewildered-looking young man is trying to pick out a card from a display that is conveniently categorized under the following headings: Biological, Adoptive, Single, Earth, Nursing, Unfit, Unwed, and on and on. The cartoon is silly, of course, and a little sad—it portrays how we actually think about mothers, how we are informed and also limited. Imagine turning this language, then, toward students. Our language instructs our inhibitions.

Let's take a particular label from the fictional card display: Single. We've all heard the term "single mother" used over and over in a wide range of contexts, and we've likely said it ourselves. That it has a negative ring is no surprise—there is something condemnatory about it, a mildly pathological undertone, a rebuke. But what substantively does the term tell us? What is revealed and what concealed when we use it? How does it instruct us? What work does it actually do?

A woman I know interviewed people within a few-square-blocks area in a poor neighborhood on Chicago's South Side.

She reported no less than twenty-eight distinct ways—and she didn't claim that she had covered the entire territory—that people described being single mothers: living with grandparents, living with boyfriend, living with aunt, living with best friend and her child, living with same-sex partner, sister and sister's husband living next door and helping out, mother living around the corner, child's father paying rent, and on and on. A few felt abandoned by men, a few others liberated from them; some were doing well, others not so well; a few had adopted children or were their legal guardians, and one said, "I chose to be a mother without a life-partner—I'm single by choice." The variety is dazzling, the scope and range and meanings seemingly endless. Women were happy and sad, optimistic and despairing, energetic and engaged moms as well as alienated and reluctant ones. This complexity is swept away with the lazy label "single mother": the rough edges sanded off, the differences homogenized and stuffed into a simple gray bag. It is difficult to see this when the blinders are being applied, in this case, hidden in the policing language of social science. We utter the term over and over—single mother, single mother—as if it points to one specific condition, something objective, immutable. Our eyelids are heavy, our eyes glaze over, and before long we're completely in the hands of the carnival hypnotist.

A friend of mine who spent time in federal prison has been campaigning to abolish from job applications what she calls "the box"—that small insidious square that invites a job seeker to inform a potential employer about whether or not the applicant has had a criminal conviction. The "box" is what prisoners call the punishment cell, being put in isolation is to be "put in the box." In my friend's work the box functions as metaphor—the box is confinement, containment, constraint, control, repression, limitation, and exclusion.

When any former prisoner sees the box, it initiates an anxious inner debate: Do I check it honestly and then miss the chance for work? Do I lie, and maybe get a month or two of wages before they find out and I get fired? And what has checking this box got to do with my ability to be a barber or an animal control agent?

My friend asks how many times the term "ex-offender" can be used before the human being before you disappears and all you see is an object. When she and a group of reformers met with the Congressional Black Caucus, one well-meaning congressman referred to the group as "ex-offenders" six times before one of the activists spoke up: "Excuse me, sir, but if you call one of us an ex-offender one more time I'm going to start referring to you as 'that Negro gentleman.' You'll see that even that benign label will begin to erase your humanity."

My students tend to teach in poor urban communities, places where most people live below the government-defined poverty line. When I asked a graduate class recently to jot down words that described "poverty," they uniformly wrote about pitiable conditions: dilapidated housing, wretched neighborhoods, rats, gangs, crime, and drugs. Not only did the words lack detail, spark, intimacy, or nuance, they were mostly clichés, echoes from the mesmerizing drone of the nightly news or the calcified, received thinking of social scientists. "Poverty" instructed inhibitions, structured a common response.

I gathered an interesting counterpoint to the descriptive lists made by these graduate students from a group of young men locked in a juvenile facility, locked, as well, inside the objectified language of the powerful, for all of these kids were from families living far below the poverty line. Their words describing poverty included: police, landlords, cash exchange, crummy schools, lousy teachers, no jobs, no money. While my university students had chosen cool, distancing words that described the effects of poverty, my delinquent students generated hot words from inside the experience, words that pointed, in their minds, at least, to causes.

I later asked my graduate students how many, in the last month, had sat down to dinner with someone they considered "poor." How many had gone to a party at a poor person's home, had spent an evening out with a poor person, had gone shopping or to the laundry or the barbershop with him or her. Those who had grown up poor had, but many had not, and they found the idea almost inconceivable. We had an extended dialogue, then, not so much about poverty or those afflicted by it, but about how much of our thinking is untroubled by facts, experience, or knowledge, how comfortably it floats along on clouds of ignorance and presumption, how contented we can become in our balkanized credulity.

This is what we know: Every human being is unfinished. Every one of us is in process, in motion, in medias res—moving from place to place, from here to there, migrating, sometimes in patterns and sometimes not, growing, sent into exile on a certain day and on another day returning, learning, changing, seeing old things in surprising new ways, entering strange rooms, coming out, taking right and wrong turns, lost and then found and then lost again, meeting new people, passing through, riding on a bus or a train or a truck or a plane or—best of all, because we move at the speed of human reaction, unencumbered by steel and glass—a bicycle, drawing right and wrong conclusions, finding something, losing something else, practicing, reaching, missing, stretching, going, going, going. This is what we know of human beings: We are incomplete, and we are aware of our incompleteness. We are on a voyage, on the make and on the move.

The teacher who honors this defining incompleteness senses intuitively that to label a student is wrong in both senses of the word: it is immoral, and it is hopelessly stupid, wildly inaccurate. It is immoral to reduce a human being to an object. It is stupid to try to flatten a three-dimensional, darting, thrusting figure into a one-dimensional thing, because it creates a grotesque misrepresentation: to his community Harold may be a generous helper, but to the school he is a "reluctant reader"; among her friends Luz is known as an artist and a creative spirit, at school she is reduced to an acronym, BD (behavior disordered); all around the city Harp is an admired poet, at school he is ADHD (attention deficit hyperactivity disordered). Something is out of focus, out of balance in these lopsided labels and judgments.

All of us are actors and subjects, stars of our own lives; each of us is our very own author and inventor, agent and manager, director, curator, coordinator, chief of operations. Each human being is a project, and the human project is a project of inquiry conducted in the world and with one another, a project of restlessness and relentlessness, a ceaseless struggle to know and to be—the primal struggle that begins at birth and only ends with death. We seek the truth; we want to be free.

Students burst into classrooms with energy and desire and intention. Each brings a voice, a set of experiences and knowledge and know-how, a way of seeing and thinking and being. Each, again, is an unruly spark of meaning-making energy on a voyage of discovery.

Right away the lessons of school try to assert themselves—lessons about obedience and conformity, about hierarchy and one's place in it, about the suppressing of desire and the delaying of satisfaction, about boredom, irrelevance, meaninglessness. If the lessons begin to take, the life is being sucked out of students. The structure of school, the expectations and the dailiness of regular routines and traditions and assumptions will have accomplished something sinister: students become arid, flat, opaque. They arrived vivid and propulsive, full of color, noise, and life, but now they are still and lifeless, unseen, unheard, invisible even to themselves. The late Lillian Weber, champion of children at the Workshop Center for Open Education at the City College of New York, once said: "They begin school an exclamation point and a question mark; too often they leave as a plain period." This is what teachers who teach toward freedom oppose.

Making students invisible is a singular accomplishment. It is aided by tests and grades that function more as autopsies than diagnostics, the well-meaning but entangling ideology of providing "services," the fragmentation of the curriculum, all manner of myths and half-truths and received thinking about students and their communities.

A commitment to the visibility of students as persons requires a radical reversal: teachers, whatever else they do, must become students of their students. The student becomes a source of knowledge and information and energy, actor, speaker, creator, constructor, thinker, doer—a teacher as well as a learner. Together students and teachers explore, inquire, investigate, search, ask questions, criticize, make connections, draw tentative conclusions, pose problems, act, seek the truth, name this and that phenomenon, circle back, plunge forward, reconsider, gather steam, pause, reflect, reimagine, wonder, build, assert themselves, listen carefully, speak, and so on.

This reversal, this dialectic, is recognized by any teacher who is paying attention. Plato saw it, and so did Rousseau. In *Democracy and Education,* John Dewey, speaking about shared activity, said, "The teacher is a learner, and the learner is, without knowing it, a teacher—and upon the whole, the less consciousness there is, on either side, of either giving or receiving instruction, the better."

Becoming a student of her students, the teacher opposes the manipulative reduction of their lives into neatly labeled packages. She resists both the easy embrace of oversimplified identities—a reliance on a single aspect of a life to say it all—and the erosive gesture of fragmenting lives into conceptually crude categories. Her stance is identification *with,* not identification *of,* her students. Her approach is solidarity, not service.

This does not mean that the teacher busies herself with knowing everything about her students while avoiding knowing anything at all about herself. Hers is not the stance of surveillance; she is not the undercover cop wearing a wire. She is side by side, hand in hand, working in concert with her students to know the world and, if necessary, to change it. Teachers must commit to know themselves as they, too, change and grow.

The teacher takes a step out from behind the desk, away from the lectern, off the pedestal, and perhaps off the cliff.

There is a feeling of vertigo as the teacher looks with new eyes, as the familiar is made strange. There is risk and there is fear —hard work, this never ending attentiveness, this improvisation—but there is satisfaction as well. She frees herself from the terror of teaching. She no longer has to pretend to be a god, all knowing, all powerful, beneficent one minute, punishing the next. She can shed the hypocrisy and phoniness of the teacher pose and begin to face herself as she really is. She can discover her students as they really are, too, and recognize that there is always more to know in all directions. Who in the world are they?

Making a commitment to the humanity of our students is in the first place an act of faith—we do not require our students to prove their three-dimensionality to us in situations that diminish and contain them, but instead we accept their humanity as the "evidence of things not seen." It is also an explicit act of resistance—resistance to the machinery of labeling that characterizes the modern predicament in all areas and has become endemic and relentless in the realm of schools, resistance to the reduction of humanity into categories. The toxic habit of labeling is increasingly the lingua franca of schools; without labels, it seems, the whole edifice would simply collapse.

When I began teaching in the 1960s we were told earnestly that some of our students were "culturally deprived"—it was spoken of as if it were a condition, like cancer or freckles. We were to identify the culturally deprived among our students and offer specific help to cure them. I remember the First Lady, Lady Bird Johnson, in those days campaigning for Head Start—which was and is a wonderful program—always steeping her efforts in the language of cultural deprivation: We need to rescue children, she would say, from islands of nothingness, and bring them into the human family.

At the White House tea during which Head Start was formally inaugurated, the First Lady was stretching to underline the urgency of her favored program: Do you know, she said a little breathlessly, I met a five-year-old boy in Texas recently who didn't even know his own name. The well-fixed assembled in the room gasped, but every teacher imagined the scene differently: a community center in the ghetto, the crush of reporters and cameramen pushing down the corridor, the lights, the noise, and in the middle of the crowd the brightly lit First Lady surrounded by muscle in suits—What's your name, honey? she asks sweetly, bending toward the boy. I dunno, mumbles the kid, an entirely appropriate response for a five-year-old confronting a stranger and a crowd, a response transformed and then employed as evidence of palpable backwardness, real stupidity.

It didn't take long for insightful educators to rise up against the language of deficit and despair, of Lady Bountiful and noblesse oblige and the white man's burden. Thoughtful people observed that deprivation of wealth and opportunity was serious, but not an internal condition; people pointed out that Spanish was not a lesser language than English. "Cultural deprivation" as a commonsense category disappeared from use.

Yet the hope for a more holistic and robust and vivid understanding of children as living, breathing, trembling creatures was short-lived. The explosion of tags and labels and categories goes on and on: "learning disabled," "behavior disordered," "gifted and talented." A particularly irritating and unhelpful label is the ever present "at risk." We have all heard it; most of us have even uttered it. Sometimes it seems that "at risk" is somewhere in the air we breathe in schools. I asked a scholar who had given a paper entitled "At Risk in the Kindergarten" to give me a simple working definition of "at risk" as it applies to kindergartners, leaving aside all the insider research lingo: Oh, he said, simple: poor, single-mother home, African American or immigrant, peer-influenced. Sounds like "culturally deprived," I said. Yes, he responded, but we don't use that term anymore. Perfect, I thought. Progress.

"At risk" adds an authenticating medical dimension to a description and a prescription made long before any real investigation begins. We talk widely of cancer risks and the risk factors for AIDS, and here social scientists—white coated and somber like their medical comrades—attach the identical language to a specific group of schoolchildren and their families. Society in this scenario is unquestionably healthy and well except for an invasion of "at risk" microorganisms; children carry the social disease; we must act boldly, scientifically, and in the best interest of the patient. Symptoms include a range of manifestations (teenage pregnancy, single-parent, mother-headed household) but the decisive indicators must be being poor and black, because any of the other symptoms applied to a white, middle-class professional, for example, are seen as a choice, a temporary aberration, or something other than justification for membership in the "at risk" group.

This, then, is all something of a hoax, or a kind of voluntary group madness. If everyone sees evidence of witchcraft, there must be witches. In our society today, "at risk" functions as a kind of witch-hunting metaphor: it is a label in search of some verifying content, offering a thin surface of scholarship and pseudoscience to cover the thickest and most persistent stereotypes about poor and African American people. The label falls conveniently in step with contemporary political and policy priorities: it blames poor people for poverty and sanctions findings that locate character and behavioral defects inside individuals—without searching out and exploring any corresponding structural problems within society or the economic system.

To the well meaning, it is an unfortunate fate that simply befalls some people; to the mean-spirited, the bogeymen are black people themselves. While poverty was once an act of God and proof of a morally defective character (and this attitude persists in some circles), then considered an act of biology and proof of poor genes (this rationale is making a strong comeback), today the hip, sophisticated observer attributes the problem to "a culture of poverty." This strikes me as the ascendancy of mystifying, quack social science.

While everyone wants to "help" the children "at risk," that help breaks down into two large camps. One is a kind of entangling help—the more you get, the more you need and the more ensnared you become. The other is the kind of help meted out by a stern father—this beating will make you better—and includes building ever-increasing numbers of prisons. Both camps believe that they know best; neither would think to ask youngsters or their families to define their own situations or their own needs and experiences in their own ways. Being "at risk" apparently disqualifies human beings from self-awareness or meaningful social commentary.

In all my years working in a wide range of urban communities, I have never heard a person call himself or herself "at risk." It is simply not a satisfactory self-identifier (Hi, my name is Rachel, I'm at risk). This is a broad hint of what can destroy even the best of intentions. Further, it is unlikely that their logical opposites will ever catch on (the popularity of "underclass," for example, will not likely be matched by a corresponding "overclass").

In "Nikki-Rosa," a 1969 poem about growing up poor on Chicago's South Side, Nikki Giovanni ends by throwing the reductive labels back:

... and I really hope no white person ever has cause to
          write about me
because they never understand Black love is Black wealth
          and they'll
probably talk about my hard childhood and never under-
          stand that
all the while I was quite happy

There is, interestingly, an available literature that illustrates something quite different: let's call it the autobiography and memoir of children of promise. This work illuminates questions of self-naming and self-identification, and it is neither accusatory nor patronizing. This literature speaks of interior meaning-making against an external world that is seen as hard and often impenetrable. It is a literature largely ignored by scholars and policymakers precisely because it is self-authored, and yet this work—whose practitioners include Luis Rodriguez, Claude Brown, Sandra Cisneros, and James Baldwin—is rich and potentially useful. The quest in these works centers on being understood, being known, creating a name of one's own. One of the most powerful generators of this tradition is *The Autobiography of Malcolm X* (1965), a searing life story that has achieved the status of a literary classic.

For Malcolm X, early experiences of school were also the beginning of a lifelong struggle with issues of naming and self-identity:

> At five, I ... began to go to school. .... The white kids didn't make any great thing about us. .... They called us "nigger" and "darkie" and "Rastus" so much that we thought those were our natural names. .... it was just the way they thought about us.

No one saw young Malcolm as he saw himself, a whole person with a full complement of human desires, needs, hopes, dreams, aspirations, and feelings. He was a thing, a one-dimensional object, stuck in the immutable expectations of others and their essentialist, entirely predetermined universe. He was, to them, lacking in some core moral or intellectual or spiritual element that would allow him full and complete membership in the human family. Nothing personal, nothing sensible, just business as usual. Malcolm was a "nigger"—neither more nor less.

Malcolm's family was decimated after his father's death at the hands of white supremacists. Malcolm and his brothers and sisters all became "state children," wards of the court, and as always, the destruction was accomplished by well-meaning people acting on a convenient label—in this case "crazy" or "mentally unstable"—that had been applied to Malcolm's mother.

Malcolm dropped out of school. He had succeeded in getting high marks, he had been active in sports and clubs, he had even been elected class president. And yet he came to believe that school was not the path to a better life for him. He knew many people who had succeeded in school, yet still had cramped, narrow, unhappy existences. He could not connect school success with happiness or broadening his own life chances. And so Malcolm became part of the massive, largely unarticulated school-boycott movement whose members were known as dropouts.

His struggle to name himself, to create a self-identity, to become educated and visible, was only beginning. His efforts, like so many others, are captured in the words of Nina Simone's soul-stirring anthem "I Wish I Knew How It Would Feel to Be Free." She sings of a deep desire to break all the chains that bind us, that hold us one from another. She longs to speak in a voice that might awaken the whole world, that could allow each of us to know something of what it means to be another person from deep within. "Then you'd see," she croons, "and agree, that everyone should be free."

In Boston, Malcolm became known as "Detroit Red," the flamboyant, zoot-suit-wearing street hustler. And in prison, where "you never heard your name, only your number—it grew stenciled on your brain," he was the incorrigible con "Satan." Eventually he became the redeemed minister Malcolm X, the person known the world around.

Finally, shortly before his death, Malcolm X became el-Hajj Malik el-Shabazz, internationalist and revolutionary. Cut down at thirty-nine, Malcolm X's struggle for a full and powerful identity was partially realized, perhaps, in the space he created for others to name themselves with self-respect and strength.

I imagine myself a teacher in Michigan, and Malcolm X my student, a kid of ten or twelve, say, or fifteen. What would I have seen? What might I have said? What beliefs and attitudes and experiences might have instructed my imagination and my inhibition?

The labeling business has run completely amok in our schools, the proliferation getting nuttier and nuttier as it rolls along:

MED, ADD, LD, DAP, BD, TAG, GED—the whole alphabet soup. In the *Onion*, a biting satirical newspaper, a headline proclaims, "New Study Reveals Millions of American Children Suffering from YTD—Youthful Tendency Disorder." A sidebar contains the ten early warning signs of YTD, behaviors such as "talks to imaginary friend" and "subject to spontaneous outbursts of laughter." A mother is quoted as saying she was concerned to learn that her daughter had been diagnosed with YTD, but relieved to know that she herself wasn't a "bad mother."

Like all worthwhile cultural satire, this piece works because it reveals a deeper truth about the predicament we have created for ourselves. We box, we contain, we chop off. And in the process, we are, all of us, diminished.

There is an antidote to all this foolishness, but it requires vigilance, effort, and consciousness. We begin with a vow not to repeat the clichés that seem to cling to some students like barnacles, sharp and ugly. We can also try to gather examples of places where the labels are disrupted and overturned—I collect those examples and hold to them when I need a dose of hope or confidence. In the Juvenile Detention Center in Chicago, for example, I worked alongside a brilliant young teacher named Deborah Stern. Deborah built her teaching around cocreating curriculum projects with students—an approach captured in a useful book she wrote called *Teaching English So It Matters*—and I was regularly dazzled by the deeply engaged projects that were created in her classroom on a regular basis.

One curriculum unit that she cocreated with the kids focused on responsibility and choice making, an intense issue for all adolescents and of particular importance, perhaps, for kids in trouble with the law. Deborah always brought poetry to her teaching, and one typical assignment was for students to take a poem that had particular meaning or power for them and to rewrite it using their own biography as the text. In this unit on choice and its consequences, one poem she introduced was by Rainer Maria Rilke, published in 1905 (included in *Selected Poems of Rainer Maria Rilke,* 1981, translated by Robert Bly):

Sometimes a man stands up during supper and walks
      outdoors,
and keeps on walking, because of a church that stands
      somewhere
in the East.

And his children say blessings on him as if he were dead.

And another man, who remains inside his own house,
      stays there,
inside the dishes and in the glasses, so that his children
      have to go
far out into the world toward that same church, which
      he forgot.

In response, a fifteen-year-old girl, pregnant, gang involved, drug involved, wrote this:

Sometimes a woman stands up during her pregnancy
and goes to the clinic, and walks out a few hours later,
because of a future that stands somewhere
in her own mind.

And her parents and her boyfriend curse her as if
she was dead.

And another woman has the baby,
lives there, inside the diapers and days of babysitting
so that her boyfriend can go out into the world
toward a future, which she had to forget.

Whenever I read these poems in tandem, I get goose bumps—not only do I love Stern's student's poem, but there is also the chilling recognition that if she had been in my classroom I might have missed this poet. The apparent, available characteristics broadcast by her physical presence and her demeanor might have instructed my inhibitions and blinded me to the talent within.

As my time at the Juvenile Detention Center was ending, Ella Fitzgerald, the great jazz diva, passed away. The tributes were widespread and deserving, but the one that captured my eye contained a little-known fact: Ella had spent time as a teenager in a detention center in upstate New York. The enterprising reporter had tracked down Ella's English teacher from those days, now an old woman, who said wistfully, "I've thought about it all these years.... I had the great Ella Fitzgerald in my classroom, and I didn't even know it." The superintendent of the facility added, "The tragedy is that they were all Ellas"—meaning, of course, that each was a person of worth and possibility—"and we had no way to know it."

Would I have missed Ella Fitzgerald had she been in my classroom? Could I have made visible the talent in the room? How?

As five tall young men wearing colorful sneakers and starter jackets and gold chains assembled in the front row of a Chicago school auditorium as part of a celebration of reform efforts, I heard a reporter whisper to a colleague that he was sure they were Farragut High School's basketball team, destined to become state champs. When the young men were introduced a few minutes later and stood awkwardly to acknowledge the applause, they were indeed Illinois state champs—they were the Orr High School chess champions, and they had crushed the north suburban New Trier to gain the title.

Later, when I asked their coach, a math teacher, the secret of their success, he said something that has become burned into my consciousness: "I had two things in mind when I organized the chess club," he said. "First, I love these kids and I think they have minds and abilities that the school ignores. And second, I love chess." He went on to explain all the wondrous qualities of chess as my eyes glazed over. But what remains is this: If you love the kids and you allow your teaching to be powered by that love, and if you love the world, or some small part of the world—

African American poetry, physics or calculus, kites or reptiles or music—you can achieve greatness in the classroom. Wonderful lesson plans and railroad-watch regularity will not get you there. It begins with the visibility of your students.

Recently at a spoken-word gathering, after several kids had delivered—or as they said, "spit"—a range of vital and propulsive poems, three young men rolled onto the stage in heavy wheelchairs. One needed help holding his mike, one's head lolled uncontrollably. When the music began they belted out a rap about what people see and don't see when they look at them in their chairs, when their disabilities seem to trump everything else. "Forget that inhibition," they chanted, "I'm more than my condition." They shouted out to reclaim their full humanity, to resist the labels, and to insist that policy for the disabled take into account the voices of their community. The chorus, "Nothing about me without me," was taken up by the crowd, and then everyone roared the group's name, to wild applause: "Unexpected!" Who am I in this world? Unexpected. And they were.

In her 1993 lecture to the Swedish Academy as recipient of the Nobel Prize in literature, Toni Morrison spoke about the power of words to shape our lives, for good and for bad. It is words, she notes, that allow us to name ourselves and our world, to make sense of our existence, to narrate our experiences and thereby gain a modicum of control over them. "We die," she said. "That may be the meaning of life. But we do language. That may be the measure of our lives."

Morrison begins her lecture with a story about an old woman, blind but wise, who is visited by a group of children determined to mock her clairvoyance and show her to be a fraud: "They enter her house and ask the one question the answer to which rides solely on her difference from them, a difference they regard as a profound disability: her blindness."

One of the youngsters announces: "'I hold in my hand a bird. Tell me whether it is living or dead.'" The old woman's silence is long and deep, and when she finally speaks, "her voice is soft but stern . . . 'I don't know whether the bird you are holding is dead or alive,' " she tells them, " 'but what I do know is that it is in your hands.' "

The old woman is reprimanding the children, turning their mockery back upon them, asserting that it is their choice, that they are responsible for "the small bundle of life" they hold in their hands.

Morrison reinterprets this ancient folktale, taking the bird to be language, the old woman a writer, and the youngsters the forces that have the power to crush or vitalize words. Language is susceptible to erasure, can die or be killed, she says, can dominate or control: "Oppressive language does more than represent violence; it is violence; does more than represent the limits of knowledge; it limits knowledge."

The opposite is also true: language can illuminate and liberate, can allow us to name the obstacles to our humanity and open thereby possible spaces and even whole worlds for us to explore: "It arcs toward the place where meaning may lie," she says, even though it "can never live up to life once and for all." Whether it is "slender, burrowing, blasting or refusing to sanctify; whether it laughs out loud or is a cry without an alphabet, the choice word or the chosen silence, unmolested language surges toward knowledge, not its destruction." Words, the "puny inexhaustible voice, still talking" that William Faulkner evoked in his Nobel speech in 1950, are the stuff we're made of.

The old blind woman in Morrison's tale can be thought of, as well, as a teacher. Her students are mocking her limits, but she turns the provocation around. She tells the young people that their lives are in their own hands, and that they have the power to shape or destroy beyond anything she can or will do. Her silence tells them that they are responsible for themselves, that she will not pontificate or posture or pretend an authority she does not want or need, and indeed, does not have. Her patient witnessing eventually calls out their own voices, for she knows something that they must learn—there is no master narrative that settles things once and for all. There is no lesson or syllabus or course that contains the answers. Rather there are voyages, and always more fundamental questions to pursue.

Taking the side of the student can unleash a set of tensions that might induce a sense of panic, prompting us to search for a less arduous and perplexing obligation. Teachers face particular pressures to retreat when the intimate educational encounters they had hoped for seem far way, when, for example, there are too many students and too little time, stingy support and not enough resources, when our vision is blinkered because standardized ways of teaching and testing are in ascendance. Under such circumstances teachers often feel they have no choice but to abandon what seems suddenly like a romantic and unrealistic allegiance.

There are particular tensions between the teacher and the profession, the teacher and her job. "Professionalism," which can too easily come to rest upon an elitist logic and an inaccessible, coded jargon, and "career," a hierarchical exclusiveness and an often perverse structure of rewards and punishments, create distance and, inevitably, contempt. Taking the side of the student in this arena means resisting the dogma of profession and career, breaking with their seductions and enticements, understanding and accepting, therefore, the unavoidable conflict between a concern for humanity and the demands of the job. It means participating fully within a community, but remaining skeptical of it; valuing colleagues but never at the expense of an authentic connection with students. Rather than hoping to overcome this tension once and for all, teachers must resolve to live within its ambiguities and conflicts, negotiating them as they emerge.

Authentic relationships between teachers and students in schools are nearly impossible, and the fault—in spite of the clichés with which we reassure ourselves—lies partly in the structure of school and the culture of professionalism. The teacher is required to assess, evaluate, and formally judge students, but students rarely assess or judge teachers. Teachers every day make disparaging comments about this or that kid: he's lazy, he's not working hard, she's not that bright. Imagine if a student said to a teacher: You're lazy and you don't work that hard. She'd be sent to the office and charged with disrespect, even if she were absolutely dead-on right. Teachers often make judgmental statements about students' families and communities, but imagine a student saying: Something about your lack of ambition combined with your neediness makes me wonder about how you were raised.

It is a rare teacher who will ever admit to a student that another teacher is terrible, who will ever take the side of a student in a conflict with another teacher, or who will publicly call out another teacher for misbehaving with regard to students. This is why students think teachers—even the best of them—are hypocrites. This is why authentic relationships are all but impossible.

There is another basic tension, this one between the teacher and what is taught. We often have deep obligations to our various disciplines and subject matters, dedication and passion for understanding and exploring aspects of our shared world. But our dedication and passion are expressed and undertaken in light of our commitment to the distinct humanness of our students. To begin elsewhere is to break a pledge, sever a relationship, violate growth. Taking the side of students is primary, our related responsibilities, then, always contingent.

What does it mean to be human? The answers explode from a zillion places and radiate endlessly outward. We are, to some, the children of God, each created in God's image—Emerson tweaked that and called himself "a god in ruins." We are little specks of insignificant dust floating for a brief blink in an obscure corner of a small galaxy, or we are, for Protagoras, "the measure of all things." Sophocles said that human beings are "but breath and shadow, nothing more," Mark Twain that man is "the only animal that blushes . . . or needs to." We are a naked ape or a political animal, a thinking reed, an ethical savage, or all of the above.

Philip Gourevitch's staggering account of the Rwandan genocide, *We Wish to Inform You That Tomorrow We Will Be Killed with Our Families* (1998), records the events that followed a government, and an astonishing number of its ordinary citizens, imagining "that by exterminating the Tutsi people they could make the world a better place." In a short introduction Gourevitch recounts a strange encounter he had had late at night in a bar with a pygmy man. "I have a principle," the man announced by way of opening a conversation. "I believe in the principle of *Homo sapiens*. You get me?" Gourevitch guessed he meant that all humanity is one. "That is my theory," the man responded. "That is my principle." In Rwanda in that terrible time, the idea that all humanity is one is only a theory, not a fact or an obvious truth, for in the background lies the decimation of a people. And in the wider world, too, the principle is theory—the choices, chances, and treatment of the fortunate are a far cry from what the unlucky and the downtrodden can expect.

In the ironically titled "A Contribution to Statistics" (in *Poems, New and Collected, 1957–1997,* 1998), the Nobel laureate Wislawa Szymborska sums humanity up thusly:

> Out of every hundred people,
> those who always know better:
> fifty-two.
>
> Unsure of every step:
> almost all the rest.

She absurdly attaches a number to a wide range of descriptors: "always good"—four; "led to error by youth"—sixty; "harmless alone, turning savage in crowds"—more than half.

Her categories are in turn frivolous, silly, insightful, and jarring. And at the end, this:

Worthy of empathy:
ninety-nine.

Mortal:
one hundred out of one hundred—
a figure that has never varied yet.

The human condition—blessed and cursed, strange, messy, wild, and weird. It is vast and contradictory, to be sure, but it is also shared. And so Szymborska reminds us that we are each worthy of empathy, and this becomes the teacher's creed: Each is a whole person, the narrator of his or her own life; each must be treated as a person of value and consequence and worth. Incomplete, imperfect, and valuable nonetheless.

W. H. Auden writes in the 1940 poem "As I Walked Out One Evening":

"O look, look in the mirror,
    O look in your distress:
Life remains a blessing
    Although you cannot bless.

"O stand, stand at the window
    As the tears scald and start;
You shall love your crooked neighbour
    With your crooked heart."

Your crooked neighbor and your crooked heart. Perfection eludes us, but we do what we can—the effort continues, the struggle for life must go on.

In "The Pity of Love," an essay in *Tricycle* (spring 2002), the novelist Neil Gordon wrestles with a contradiction at the center of our love for and commitment to children: "From the moment of my daughter's birth," he writes, "I understood that I would fear for her the rest of my life." He then evokes W. B. Yeats's 1892 poem "The Pity of Love," which begins, "A pity beyond all telling / Is hid in the heart of love." The poet offers a list of the ordinary occurrences of daily life—the market, the clouds passing by, and the wind—and then surprises us in a last line that is both abrupt and enigmatic. All those regular things, he concludes, "Threaten the head that I love." What is the threat? "To love children deeply is *not only* to risk a catastrophic loss," Gordon writes, to "love children is also to lose them over and over again, on a daily and momentary basis, not as they die, or move away, but as they simply grow."

For Gordon this "shocking fact" of loss, not as accident but rather as "part of the very identity of love," leads to a deeper recognition of "the full meaning of impermanence," and the occasion to realize again that "our children are our teachers." Hierarchy is undone; children teach us not just about themselves but, importantly, about ourselves as well. In this Gordon cites Yeats's greatest insight about "the inseparability of process and identity." In Yeats's poem "Among School Children" (1927), it is achieved, interestingly, in a classroom. The poem ends:

> O chestnut-tree, great rooted blossomer,
> Are you the leaf, the blossom or the bole?
> O body swayed to music, O brightening glance,
> How can we know the dancer from the dance?

Gordon reflects on the little lies we tell children to provide them the illusion of safety and permanence, to protect them from the worst of life and the inevitable in life, but, he adds, "there is no lie as bad as when we whitewash the possibility of freedom, of happiness." Happiness is, of course, tied to "the practice of freedom," which is neither easy nor automatic, but "frightening and difficult." The "pity beyond all telling" can challenge us to move beyond the illusion of safety, and also beyond the illusion of danger. It can instruct us to live our lives with children as if each moment matters, each is its own eternity. The important thing is to push forward, to live.

* * *

What does it mean to be human? What does it mean to create and maintain our humanity in the face of dehumanization? What does it mean to teach in a human community?

We have agreed as a matter of public policy that people in wheelchairs in Chicago, for example, are fully human, and that our public restrooms and city buses must be built to reflect that fact. This rather recent agreement, remember, is the result of the sustained, militant struggle of the disabled themselves and their allies. "Nothing about us without us," they shouted as they blocked doorways and fought for a more inclusive understanding of humanity than had existed until they spoke up.

There is a delightful movement in architecture and design that takes this a step further—the movement is called "universal design." With universal design, "wheelchair-accessible" signs on specialized restroom stalls are no longer necessary, because every stall is made roomy, comfortable, and accessible to all. Revolutionary, no? Height-adjustable drinking fountains, gently sloping ramps, "easy grip" utensils—each of these is sensible, sustainable, and accessible, each a benefit to everyone, removing the stigma of "otherness" and the isolating categories of "normal" and "disabled." They are designed for equitable and flexible use, simple and intuitive use, incorporating a high tolerance for individual differences. They humanize the built environment for everyone.

To be human is to be on a voyage, to be a project, imagining, reaching, changing oneself and the world. Having a mind capable of projecting, choosing, reflecting—this is the human signature that teachers both seek and nourish. Becoming students of our students provides a compass and a guide. Young children and babies are great fun to be with precisely because they are the least dogmatic of human beings—they are constantly experimenting, forever making unique connections, always open to discovery and surprise. Far from passive or inert, they are going, going, going. We can with some effort relearn this approach from them.

Adolescents, too—struggling to claim the world for themselves, to name their own ideals about life and living, and noisily disillusioned with the grown-up world, which is to them too often a hypocritical, empty, compromised, and false world—can be helpful guides. They are lively, impatient, diverse, tumultuous, intense idealists clamoring for authenticity, qualities too often squashed in classrooms. Adolescents are eager to make a mark: "I shall create!" Gwendolyn Brooks wrote in the 1968 poem "Boy Breaking Glass," "If not a note, a hole. / If not an overture, a desecration." Teachers who see this tension at work can provide an environment that opens the creative vent, the inventive mind, the productive option, openings that allow for alternatives to be seen and chosen and for destructive routes to be challenged and even closed.

We seem almost always to respond to teenagers with an authoritarianism in the name of clarity and standards. For example, "zero tolerance" has become a favorite phrase in schools, promoted as clarifying what might have been perceived as murky, ambiguous. It is odd, though: there is no murkiness at all in my thoughts on drug abuse, for example. I think that cigarettes are toxic, alcohol poisonous—heavier drugs are even worse—and so I don't use them, and I strongly disapprove of their use. What does saying that I have "zero tolerance" for them add? It sounds appropriately tough, perhaps, but what would I do, for example, what action would I take if I saw someone abusing alcohol? Kill them? Jail them? Punch them out? Expel them? Sounding tough is quite a different thing from acting wisely to educate young people. And since contexts and circumstances are always specific and often complex, wise prescriptions will likely be various.

Furthermore, saying I have "zero tolerance" for alcohol gives it an oddly privileged position. How much tolerance do I have for sexual abuse? For bigotry? Intolerance or disrespect? Meanness or thoughtlessness? Well, it is clear that these are complicated. "Zero tolerance" simplifies, closes the door to conversation.

Move into more complicated issues and the need for conversation only intensifies. Young people, in particular, need steady, reasonable grown-ups to talk to, to think with, to bounce back off of. Closing the door is a form of abandonment, of neglect.

We should refine our standard and ask, What if this were my child? The question cannot be about some abstract child, every child, the mob of children. That turns other people's children into things, objectifies them. To ask, Is it good enough for my child?—not, Is it a perfect arrangement for my child?—is to begin to set limits of acceptability. Personalizing our approach to juveniles does not mean that there are no serious consequences to action or behavior, but it does remind us that a child who breaks the law will return to society someday, and that among our central goals must be recovery. It reminds us that our efforts on behalf of our children and other people's children must include cleaning up their environment—removing adult-controlled toxic elements like guns and drugs—and a sustained struggle to provide productive work, decent schools, and community centers to support and challenge them, to engage their hopes and dreams and capacities. We must fight for the obvious: a child in crisis, a child in trouble, is still a child.

When Gwendolyn Brooks passed away, there was a moving, daylong memorial celebrating her life and her work at the University of Chicago's Rockefeller Chapel, where family and friends honored her contribution to literature and to humanity. She had been poet laureate of Illinois for many years, an engaged intellectual and a public citizen, a teacher with a huge following of students and admirers. On that day Anthony Walton, one of her students, read a poem he had written for the occasion called simply "Gwendolyn Brooks (1917–2000)":

> Sometimes I see in my mind's eye a four-or five-
> year-old boy, coatless and wandering
> a windblown and vacant lot or street in Chicago

on the windblown South Side. He disappears
but stays with me, staring and pronouncing
me guilty of an indifference more callous
than neglect, condescension as self-pity.

Then I see him again, at ten or fifteen, on the corner,
Say, 47th and Martin Luther King or in a group
of men surrounding a burning barrel off Lawndale,
everything surrounding vacant or for sale.
Sometimes I trace him on the train to Joliet
or Menard, such towns quickly becoming native
ground to these boys who are so hard to love, so hard
to see, except as case studies.

Poverty, pain, shame, one and a half million
dreams deemed fit only for the most internal
of exiles. That four-year-old wandering
the wind tunnels of Robert Taylor, of Cabrini
Green, wind chill of an as yet unplumbed degree—
a young boy she did not have to know to love.

Anthony Walton, honoring Gwendolyn Brooks's approach
to her art and her people, evokes the less visible and yet somehow central dimensions of our work—ethical dimensions embedded in the enterprise of education—from several different
angles of regard: from that of the four- or five-year-old boy, coat-
less and wandering; from the perspective of that ten- or fifteen-
year-old on the corner; from the standpoint of the human cargo
on a train destined for the cage. He nails the point of view of an
adult world caught up in other matters, indifferent in part, and
where engaged, guided by theories and standards that are simply inadequate to capture the complexity of lived life—those
busy, blinding case studies. But then, suddenly, that surprising
and oh-so-hopeful denouement: "a young boy she did not have
to know to love." What characterizes Brooks's body of work, and

the meaning of this poem for teachers, is the invitation to look at children, at mothers and fathers and brothers and sisters, as more than shadows, more than disappearing traces on a page.

There are millions of kids who feel that they have no future. What do we really know of them? What is to become of them? What are their choices and their chances? Other kids feel that they are worthy to be here—feeling that, the world becomes their oyster. What's the difference? What do the kids of hope have that the others lack? How do you bring these affirmations of hope to your classroom?

With an allegiance to our students, we find ourselves drawn into families and communities. Our commitment stretches. We take their side, too, the side of humanity. This stance draws energy, sustenance, and direction from taking the side of our students, and it branches out. As it radiates away from the homeroom, from the class and the school, the classroom functions as a kind of atlas to the larger world. If, for example, in our classrooms we insist that every student is a three-dimensional creature much like ourselves, with hopes, dreams, aspirations, skills, desires, and so on, if every student is treated with awe and reverence in recognition that each is the one and only, each a universe of one, then we carry that practice outward, we extend it, and we insist that every single human life, even those we will never know, is sacred, each of incalculable value. If we develop a stance in our classrooms based on the faith that every student can learn, can grow, can change, then we operate in the world beyond with that same principle intact—every person can learn and can grow, each of us is capable of change, each is a work in progress. Being student centered, we can learn to become family centered and community centered. In fact, we can't really be student centered until we are family centered, community centered, person centered.

José Saramago reflects on the meaning of a name—and the power of a life—in his 1999 novel *All the Names*, the story of Senhor José, a lowly clerk in the Central Registry of Births, Marriage and Deaths in an unnamed city. Senhor José is ordinary in every way—graying and slight, modest in his appetites, restrained or, perhaps more accurately, repressed, meager, a man of routines and habits, regulation and order. He questions nothing, accedes to anything, conforms completely. For Senhor José the troubling *why* of his life has never arisen—he measures his days at the copying desk, nibbles at his mousy meals, retires to his dreary room, the same each night. His is the unexamined life in full.

Senhor José accepts, of course, the importance and the majesty of the Central Registry—its motto is, after all, "All the Names." Here all of humanity is aligned in a towering and inexorably growing archive, records stretching back to the beginning and, with people continually being born, coupling, and dying, arcing forward as well. It is itself a kind of living thing, reflecting a daily "border conflict," "an embarrassing fringe of confusion," between the cards of the living and the cards of those already dead, and issuing forth a "muffled sound" that rises and falls "like a distant bellow." Senhor José and his fellow clerks are the defenders of order in the threatening face of chaos. Only later will José discover that "All the Names" is the motto, as well, of the General Cemetery, and that the clerks there consider the Central Registry as a mere tributary. There is a kind of simple symmetry to the work.

In his perfect predictability, in his unremarkable suit of armor, Senhor José has a single chink: he secretly gathers news clippings of famous people, limiting his collection to just one hundred luminaries. Like other collectors, he "cannot bear the idea of chaos being the one ruler of the universe" and so attempts "to impose some order on the world," a task that can be managed only so long as the collection is defended.

One night he decides—quite out of character and for reasons he himself cannot fathom—to enter the Central Registry surreptitiously in order to copy out the objective information from the cards of his celebrities, the documentary proof of their existence. In the imposing darkness, surrounded by musty files piled to the ceiling, he experiences "a feeling of confidence that he had never before experienced in his entire life." His transgression is exhilarating—he sits in the registrar's high chair, and he stays there till dawn. Senhor José has changed fundamentally and across the board—he is a new person. To his astonishment, no one at work the next day even notices. He is underground, a fugitive.

And so the transgressions proceed, and on a fateful night, in his haste to pilfer five more celebrity cards for his collection, he returns home with a sixth, the intrusive card of an unknown woman, which had become stuck to one of the others. Curious, he studies the card of this woman until, as is his inclination, he becomes obsessed—here is a person with "the same beginning as everyone else," but who will never be written about nor noticed nor become an entry anywhere but in the Central Registry and then the General Cemetery. Why? he wonders. Why is her life "like a cloud that passes without leaving behind it any trace of its passing," anonymous, unacknowledged—"Like me, thought Senhor José"? He imagines his one hundred famous people with their titles and appellations on one end of a scale, the unknown woman on the other, and is "surprised to discover that all of them together weighed no more than this one, that one hundred equaled one, that one was worth as much as a hundred." The unknown woman leads Senhor José on an odyssey into the darkness, a voyage of further transgression, deeper discovery, and surprise as he works to untangle a single life, that precious and precarious "vine . . . situated between two voids." Finding one three-dimensional creature, of course, provides a template for finding another and then another, and eventually oneself. This is every teacher's potential passage.

The aim of the teacher who teaches toward freedom, again, is to recognize that all children are unruly sparks of meaning-making energy, always dynamic, constantly in motion, and forever on a journey. Who in the world am I? You are an entire universe, and you are one part of the great sea that is all of us. We do well to remember, as well, our own quests and journeys, our own meaning making. Our first commitment, then, is this: to recognize and call out the humanity in each of our students. We become students of our students. We take their side.

3. Building a Republic of Many Voices
WHERE IS MY PLACE IN THE WORLD?

Stokely Carmichael was a freedom school teacher in Mississippi in the early 1960s, long before he became nationally known as the fiery leader of the Student Nonviolent Coordinating Committee (SNCC). Freedom schools were set up to help young people develop a sense of agency and power in order to participate fully in the movement that was shaking the South and changing people's lives. Stokely began one class by writing two sets of sentences on the board:

I digs wine	*I enjoy drinking cocktails*
The peoples wants freedom	*The people want freedom*
I wants to reddish to vote	*I want to register to vote*

Stokely asked the students what they thought of the two sets of sentences. One student said "peoples" didn't sound right. Stokely asked if they knew what "peoples" meant, if they knew anyone who said "peoples." Several students replied that everyone knew what it meant, and that they knew many people, including themselves, who sometimes said "peoples." But, added one, it isn't "correct English." Stokely then asked who decides what is correct and incorrect, and this exchange followed:

STOKELY: *You all say some people speak like on the left side of the board. Could they go anywhere and speak that way? Could they go to Harvard?*

CLASS: *Yes...No.*

STOKELY: *Does Mr. Turnbow speak like on the left side?*

Class: *Yes.*

STOKELY: *Could Mr. Turnbow go to Harvard and speak like that?* "I wants to reddish to vote."

CLASS: *Yes.*

STOKELY: *Would he be embarrassed?*

CLASS: *Yes...No!*

ZELMA: *He wouldn't be, but I would. It doesn't sound right.*

STOKELY: *Suppose someone from Harvard came to Holmes County and said, "I want to register to vote?" Would they be embarrassed?*

ZELMA: *No.*

STOKELY: *Is it embarrassing at Harvard but not in Holmes County? The way you speak?*

Stokely geared his teaching around posing problems and asking questions. Content was drawn from the lived experiences of students, and through dialogue, student knowledge was affirmed and acknowledged, extended and connected. Student insights were heard and respected—their lives affirmed—as important starting points toward deeper and wider ways of knowing.

The class stopped soon after this discussion for lunch, but not before Stokely asked the students to think about what constitutes a society and who makes the rules. Students noted that although most people spoke some form of "incorrect English," the "correct English" minority had a monopoly on jobs, money, and prestige. The students left the classroom wrestling with important questions about language, culture, control, politics, and power. (See W. C. Ayers, "We Who Believe in Freedom Cannot Rest Until It's Done," *Harvard Educational Review* 59, no. 4 [1989]: 520–28.)

* * *

Education is animated by the deepest and most difficult human concerns—What does it mean to be human, anyway? What is my place in the world? What kind of world can we imagine and work toward? Teaching, as I have argued, is always at bottom *for* something and *against* something else; that is, teaching occupies *contested space*. Fundamentally, teaching operates in the service of knowledge and liberation—of humanization—but it can as easily be twisted to the domain of dehumanization.

Classroom ethics, a down-to-earth, rough-and-tumble affair, comes to life when teachers struggle to open their eyes, to see the world before them as dynamic and complex, and then to make hard choices between real alternatives. Teachers who commit to teaching toward freedom find themselves thrust into a field of conflict, hope, and struggle. This often painful, lonely, always difficult work can be accomplished best by teachers who have a sense of themselves as moral agents, ethical actors, thinking people grounded in commitments that they can call upon to guide them through the unpredictable and often treacherous terrain of schools. Moral commitments operate on a different level and, ironically, on a firmer ground than, say, skills or even dispositions of mind.

The first commitment a teacher teaching toward freedom —a freedom teacher—makes is a pledge to take the side of the student—we recognize, support, and appeal to the full humanity of each. We advocate for knowledge and liberation. We become students of our students. A second, closely linked commitment is to create a space where a republic of many voices might come to life, the "uniculture" opposed, and the suffocating sameness of the domineering voice resisted. The freedom teacher vows to build an environment where human beings can face one another authentically and without masks, a place of invitation, fascination, interest, and promise. The focus here is on the environment for learning; the physical space, of course, and also, perhaps more important, the spiritual and ethical and intellectual and social spaces that only a teacher can ignite.

With one eye fixed firmly on the humanity of our students, we now turn an eye to the concentric circles of context in which students and teachers find themselves and encounter one another. What ideas and values are worked up in the environments we construct? As the architects of classroom spaces, how do we embody, display, and create spaces for the enactment of those ideas and values? What methods and approaches are consistent with affirming the humanity of our students?

The environment is the critical variable that classroom teachers can discern, critique, build, and rebuild to everyone's advantage. The environment must challenge and nurture the wide range of students who actually appear in our classrooms, with multiple entry points toward learning and a range of routes to pursue meaning. The teacher builds the context; the teacher's values, instincts, and experiences are visible in the learning environment. It is essential to reflect on our values, our expectations, and our standards, bearing in mind that the dimensions we work with are measured not just in feet and inches, but also in hopes and dreams realized, in moral reflection and ethical possibilities enacted. Think about what one senses when walking through the door: What is the atmosphere? What quality of experience is anticipated? What technique is dominant? What voice will be expressed?

The environment itself is a powerful teacher. When I first started teaching, I took my five-year-olds to the Detroit Metropolitan Airport to watch the planes take off and land. I didn't have much in mind beyond an enjoyable field trip, but I soon discovered that the concourse in any airport has a message for all of us: Move this way, Keep moving, Move rapidly. Today, perhaps, there is an added dimension—Buy! Buy! Buy!—but then it was mostly Keep going.

To a five-year-old, the message of the concourse is simple: "Run!" It took me three field trips to realize that my instructions—stick together, hold hands, don't run—were consistently overruled by the dominant voice of the environment.

What does the environment say? How can it be improved?

A fifth-grade teacher I know begins each year explaining to his students that he has only three important rules in his classroom: one, that you can chew gum—the students are amazed; two, that you can wear your hats—the boys in particular look a little ecstatic at this apparently outlaw concept; and three, that "this is a community of learners, and you must treat everyone with respect and compassion—especially when it's hard to do."

What this teacher has done in his corner of this school is to create an environment for moral reflection and ethical action. Mistakes will be made, bad behavior and thoughtless actions will occur, but undergirding all of it is a framework for learning, for embracing the teachable moment. This classroom environment is a place, in the words of the great Joe Cocker tune, of "learning to live together." Such a process goes on for a lifetime. It is a process begun in the family and potentially continued and expanded in school.

Contrast this to a posted list of rules I saw in a Chicago high school cafeteria:

No running.
No shouting.
No throwing food
No fork fights.

No fork fights? One's mind boggles, imagining the incident that led to the inclusion of that rule. Kids! Could there ever be a list adequate to capture every possible infraction lurking in the minds of high schoolers?

It's not the rules themselves that are off, of course, but what they stand for as well as what they stand against. They suggest obedience over initiative, convention over thought. Here we find conformity emphasized over morality. None of the rules invite reflection, dialogue, or judgment. Where in this environment is there a place for moral reflection, commitment, or creation? Where is there space for ethical action, or teaching toward freedom?

Imagine the unfortunate guard trying to enforce the dress code I saw posted at another Chicago high school:

No torn or too-baggy jeans.
No visible piercings beyond the face.
No starter jackets.
No boxers above the waist of pants.
No skimpy halter tops.
No dangerous jewelry.
No explicitly sexual clothing.

Visible piercings beyond the face? Dangerous jewelry? Oh, my.

The school is not aiming for greatness here. What do these rules tell young people regarding their place in the world? That it is relegated to the petty and the superficial? Could there be something more?

As far as the education of children goes, rather than teach what Natalia Ginzberg, the Italian novelist, calls "the little virtues," we might aspire to teach the great ones. Not thrift, for example, but generosity, not caution but courage, not tact but love for our neighbors, and not a longing for success but a desire to know and to be. The great virtues come from some deep and hard-to-name place, an instinct, perhaps, but it is clear that with their development the little virtues will fall into their proportionate place.

Teachers must think about the environments they create; they must examine them, reflect upon them, and then rethink and reconstruct them. What would an environment built around the great virtues look like? The preschool wizard Vivian Gussin Paley wrote a wise book called *You Can't Say You Can't Play* (1992) illuminating the central place of moral reflection and ethical action in the kindergarten. How would a teacher create a space where the great virtues were visible and available, modeled and rehearsed, enacted and demonstrated? Take the last great virtue in Ginzberg's list, a desire to know and to be. Surely a teacher with that in mind would recognize the importance of nourishing a sense of confidence and competence, feelings of self-love combined with compassion and empathy for others—to be ethical is not to be perfect, but it is to strive for awareness, to choose, to try.

In the poem "You Begin" (in *Selected Poems II: Poems Selected and New, 1976–1986*, 1987), the Canadian writer Margaret Atwood offers these instructions to a child:

> You begin this way:
> this is your hand,
> this is your eye,
> that is a fish, blue and flat
> on the paper, almost
> the shape of an eye.
> This is your mouth, this is an O
> or a moon, whichever
> you like. This is yellow.
>
> Outside the window
> is the rain, green
> because it is summer, and beyond that
> the trees and then the world,
> which is round and has only
> the colors of these nine crayons.
>
> This is the world, which is fuller
> and more difficult to learn than I have said.
> You are right to smudge it that way
> with the red and then
> the orange: the world burns.
>
> Once you have learned these words
> you will learn that there are more

words than you can ever learn.
The word *hand* floats above your hand
like a small cloud over a lake.
The word *hand* anchors
your hand to this table,
your hand is a warm stone
I hold between two words.
This is your hand, these are my hands, this is the world,
which is round but not flat and has more colors
than we can see,
It begins, it has an end,
this is what you will
come back to, this is your hand.

When Atwood writes, "You begin this way: this is your hand," she evokes a profound principle of learning: human beings learn through experience, through pushing into the world, through acting on one another and on their surroundings. To learn, one must participate. Teachers can insist on building environments worthy of student participation.

Frank R. Wilson, a neurologist, argues in the 1999 text *The Hand: How Its Use Shapes the Brain, Language, and Human Culture*, "For the brain to work it needs information that can only come from the hand acting on objects, or from tactile or kinesthetic perception." Biologically the head and the hand evolved simultaneously and in direct relation to one another. Wilson points out that early language acquisition, for example, always occurs in the company of specific motor milestones. There cannot, he asserts, be "anything called intelligence, independent of the behavior of the entire organism."

Wilson offers a kind of indictment of the schools we have built, a critique of any system that attempts to fill inert and isolated heads with information while separating them from the physical and social world we share and that we must engage in, in order to grow. In our culture we tend to draw a bright line between the mind and the body, to fragment human beings into several imagined distinct component parts, and we tend toward a hierarchy of value in which the mind sits at the top of the pyramid and the body—manual labor, physical work—lies broken off near the bottom. This set of assumptions—based on an illusion of discrete realms and separate estates—does real violence to students and to learning.

Margaret Atwood's poem—her metaphor—points us in a better direction: "This is your hand." This is your experience and your perception, your desire and your need. This is your reality. This is where we begin.

There is no imagined "right" place or time to begin a dialogue with the young—with students of any age. There is only right here, right now. You begin this way. A nursing mother can tell astonishing stories of a serious, sustained dialogue with her infant. Among other things, she will acknowledge without embarrassment or apology that she is the student, her infant the teacher. An attentive parent knows that a cry of hunger is different from a cry of discomfort or a cry of pain. When the parent responds appropriately, when he or she learns and when the infant senses that she has been heard and seen, that she has been understood, that dialogue strengthens the growing sense of herself as the main actor in her own life, a burgeoning sense of power, agency, and integrity.

At the other end of the human cycle is my mother, for example, dying of Alzheimer's disease. The last months were difficult for her as well as for my father and others of us who loved and cared for her. She was angry, often psychotic it seemed, confused, incoherent, cursing, sometimes violent. It wasn't the woman we thought we knew. Still, with my early-childhood background and teacher's spirit, I tried to listen and to respond. After all, it was she who was experiencing the disease; the best I could do was to be an honest witness and a student of her encounter with Alzheimer's. You begin this way. We had our moments. For example, she often raged against the people we saw on our drives together, calling them "pukes" and "fuckys," words she invented and applied to most people and a range of situations. I learned that if I simply noted that I had heard what she'd said, if I responded, for example, "You think he's a puke," or "Sometimes we all act a little fucky," she calmed down immediately, saying, "Well, I'm glad *someone* understands me."

Think of teaching reading to a young child, a non-English-speaking immigrant, or an illiterate adult. There is a way to teach reading that hammers away as at a wall—the teacher knows everything and the student knows nothing, the teacher is active and the student passive, the teacher is beneficent and the student resistant, the teacher emphasizes the difficulty of learning and the student acquiesces. The student may learn some day to read, but the hidden lessons are powerful, lasting, and in some ways overshadowing: the teacher knows better, learning is passive, reading is hard and unpleasant. There is, of course, an alternative, a way to work so that when the student begins reading independently it is a bit anticlimactic, practically a nonevent. This happens when students are encouraged to write their own scripts, construct their own knowledge, name their own worlds.

My son Malik teaches second-language learners in high school in California. Each of his students has mountains to climb in terms of vocabulary, grammar, syntax, usage. This describes a place he knows he has to go, but it is not where he chooses to begin, nor where he stays. Class begins with a "free write," a time for students to think, create, laugh, sometimes cry, but always to create their own texts for further work and refinement. "Today I want you to write a reflection for ten minutes on the phrase 'People always ask me,'" Malik says as he writes the words on the board. The response is electrifying: short stories and personal essays, poems and lists and cartoons. Some are serious, some earnest, others comical and full of fancy. Malik then spends time with students editing, correcting, instructing.

Malik has over twenty different languages in his classroom. "I have to figure out how to honor the home culture, the home language," he says, "while not settling for separation." He brought in a tape recorder and had his kids tell their life stories in any language they wanted—but they had to do it in just thirty seconds. He challenges, but he tries to nourish his students in the same gesture. "Everyone has to find their own way into a text," he points out.

Malik encourages his students to teach him words, meanings, customs, and he insists that they correct his mispronunciations of their names. "That's pretty basic," he says. Malik frequently asks his students: "Are there things I should know?" "Are there things I shouldn't do?" "Are there things I need to do better?"

Fundi, a 1983 documentary film by Joanne Grant, takes its name from the Swahili word for a person who masters a craft and passes it on—a *fundi* is a teacher or a storyteller, someone who gathers strength, energy, and wisdom from a whole community and then reflects those qualities back for others to use. *Fundi* was the name given to Ella Baker by the young militants of SNCC during the civil rights movement of the 1960s, and Grant's film illustrates why this largely unsung hero of the movement was considered *teacher* by leaders from Stokely Carmichael to Martin Luther King Jr., from Eleanor Holmes Norton to Bernice Reagon.

In 1960 college students began a dramatic series of sit-ins at a segregated lunch counter in Greensboro, North Carolina. Day after day, quiet and dignified, they walked into the store, sat down, and asked to be served. Day after day they were refused. Day after day a howling racist crowd spat at them, threw food on them, threatened and often beat them. And day after day they were arrested and hauled off to jail. "We were scared to death," one student said. "But we believed we were right."

Sit-ins at segregated facilities spread like wildfire throughout the South, and Ella Baker, who was then executive director of King's Southern Christian Leadership Conference (SCLC), suggested that those involved hold a meeting to assess the situation and decide what needed to be done. Baker was the oldest by decades as well as the most experienced person in the room, but she encouraged others to speak and to lead. She spoke up only one time with force: there had been pressure from the National Association for the Advancement of Colored People (NAACP), from the Congress of Racial Equality (CORE), and even from the SCLC for the students to affiliate with one of them as their youth organization, and Baker urged them to resist. "Keep the special thing separate," she advised, for she saw the courage and creativity of the young, the willingness to take on new challenges in exciting new ways, as an antidote to becoming stuck in the old and letting history pass by. Baker believed that fundamental change was necessary to create a just society: "We are going to have to learn to think in radical terms," she said. "I use the term radical in its original meaning—getting down to and understanding the cause."

In 1964 SNCC led the effort to break segregation in Mississippi through the creation of freedom schools and a massive voter-registration project called Mississippi Summer. When James Chaney, Andrew Goodman, and Mickey Schwerner went to Philadelphia, Mississippi, to look at a burned-out church that was to have served as a freedom school, they were kidnapped and murdered by organized racists as a warning to other volunteers: Stay out of Mississippi! The response was the opposite: the killings galvanized the determination, courage, and urgency of the struggle, and Mississippi was flooded with volunteers. At a memorial service for the three, Ella Baker, trembling with anger, cried out: "Until the killing of black mothers' sons becomes as important as the killing of a white mother's son, we who believe in freedom cannot rest."

The students in SNCC transcended what was expected of them—the preoccupation with individual success, career, and mobility—threw off their timid and striving upbringings, and exiled themselves to the cotton fields and farm communities of the South. They became students of the poor, the workers, the peasants. In a sense they humbled themselves, but simultaneously and in a truer sense, they enlarged themselves. There is so much to learn, they told themselves, so much to gain, so much more to become.

Freedom schools were sites of community education based on a process designed to open doors, open minds, open possibilities—an education that would enable people to surpass limitations. "Our objective is justice," Ella Baker argued. "Your life has been limited—both white and black—by racism." The opening of possibilities in life, the transformation, begins with the identification of limitations and the willingness to act against them. "No human being relishes being sat upon," she insisted, and the natural human resistance to oppression must find an effective organized form: "Nobody will do for you what you have the power to do and fail to do." Both education and freedom require self-activity, each requires the complex interplay of individual choice and assertion combined with collective action and interaction.

This kind of enabling education opposes fear, ignorance, and helplessness by strengthening knowledge and ability. It enables people to question, to wonder, and to look critically. It can be both the process by which people discover and develop various capacities as they locate themselves historically, and the vehicle for moving forward and breaking through limitations. Its singular value is that it is education for freedom.

The activist Septima Clark, educational director of the Highlander Folk School in Tennessee, applied these fundamental lessons about teaching to the huge task of educating a whole community, creating citizenship schools as part of voter-registration drives throughout the South. As a young teacher on Johns Island, South Carolina, Clark had known that the spoken language of the Carolina Sea Islands was a unique creation of the early slaves. While the islanders understand English, their own language is Gullah, a mix of the languages native to the captured Africans and the various languages of the slave traders and imperialists.

Clark taught beginning reading by creating homemade books based on the experiences of the Johns Islanders, as recounted in her first-person narrative *Ready from Within: Septima Clark and the Civil Rights Movement* (1986), edited by Cynthia Stokes Brown:

> I wrote their stories on the dry cleaner's bags, stories of their country right around them, where they walked to come to school, the things that grew around them, what they could see in the skies. They told them to me, and I wrote them on dry cleaner's bags and tacked them on the wall.

Later, after students could read stories of their own island, she brought in books and stories that could introduce them to a world beyond their experience. These "vicarious experiences" told of "great corn fields in the Midwest where farmers made thousands of dollars," and of seals and mountains and cities. As a teacher, Septima Clark built on a foundation of what students knew, and challenged them to move from the known to the unknown. She empowered her students in two ways: by affirming their life experiences and serving as a cultural and personal mirror for them; and by opening a wider world to them, introducing them to the unknown and the unexperienced.

As she recruited people to teach in the citizenship schools, Clark began with an understanding of how her students experienced the world:

> We had a day-by-day plan, which started the first night with them talking, telling us what they would like to learn. The next morning we started off with asking them: "Do you have an employment office in your town? Where is it located? What hours is it open? Have you been there to get work?" The answers to those things we wrote down on dry cleaner's bags, so they could read them. . . .
>
> We were trying to make teachers out of people who could barely read and write. But they could teach. If they could read at all, we could teach them that c-o-n-s-t-i-t-u-t-i-o-n spells constitution. We'd have a long discussion all morning about what the constitution was.

The power of the lesson was in the content. People left the teacher-education sessions to lead their own projects of voter registration and community education, and they replicated the lessons they had learned: they discussed the problems and the needs of people in their own local communities; they posed questions ("How come the pavement stops where the black section begins?"); and they organized a process that allowed for discovery and connection. The starting points for teaching were various and complex (how the local government functions, how the sharecropping system works, how to keep a bank account and avoid being cheated), but the goals were the same: affirmation, growth, power.

In the South of Ella Baker and Septima Clark, learning to read was practically a subversive activity, an activity that many thought could change the fundamental structure of the Jim Crow system. Like the slave owner who told Frederick Douglass that reading would "unfit him to be a slave," many in the South enforced black illiteracy as a pillar of white supremacy. The citizenship schools, which paralleled the heroic efforts to educate ex-slaves during the radical period of black Reconstruction immediately following the Civil War, challenged white supremacy by teaching basic literacy, encouraging people to vote, and providing an alternative sense of what it was possible to achieve. The first citizenship school organized at Johns Island was disguised as a grocery store, "to fool white people." Reading represented power; for black people it was the power to control and to change their destiny.

Teaching toward freedom is always more a possibility than an accomplishment, more a project of people in action than a finished condition. It requires a continual identification of what is to be done, a constant process of unfolding and moving forward. The process of education, of discovery, of freedom, is not so much neat, logical, smooth, and obvious in advance; it is more often messy, rough, unpredictable, and inconsistent. It can be halting and it can be slow, but it can also become an achievement and surprise us with the suddenness and power of change.

Freedom schools were created as an alternative to the oppressive schools black children attended in Mississippi. Charlie Cobb, a twenty-year-old SNCC field secretary from Springfield, Massachusetts, and a student at Howard University, wrote a memo in late 1963 advocating the creation of summer freedom schools as an alternative to a system characterized by "a complete absence of academic freedom" and an "environment that is geared to squashing intellectual curiosity, and different thinking." Cobb thought that if breaking the racist power structure was a goal, then the movement had to build "our own institutions to replace the old, unjust, decadent ones which make up the existing power structure."

Black people in Mississippi had always been officially defined by others, not themselves. While never entirely successful, the racist structure of the South was intent on black disempowerment. Black people were talked to, but told not to talk back. They were acted upon by others, but instructed not to act in their own lives. They were disciplined and managed, told what to do and what not to do, treated as one-dimensional caricatures, without voice or choice, justice or freedom. The movement set out to change all this, and to Charlie Cobb, a new kind of school would be one vehicle for that change.

Freedom schools were designed to allow students to examine their own lived experiences, to question and explore everything around them. The schools would provide the space and resources for students to make meaning for themselves, to choose, to be purposeful moral and social agents, community participants and engaged citizens, capable of understanding and changing their circumstances and surroundings. If the air in the segregated schools was stifling, the environment of the freedom schools would be liberating, clear. "The Mississippi Freedom School Curriculum—1964," written by civil rights activists in the spring of 1963, is divided into two parts: the "Academic Curriculum" and the "Citizenship Curriculum." A third area—artistic, recreational, and cultural activities—is encouraged because "the comradeship formed on the ball field or in group singing may be the basis of your relationship with a student."

The authors of the freedom school curriculum were clear that there was no place for authoritarian teachers or didactic teaching, and that the curriculum "must necessarily be flexible": "You, your colleagues, and your students are urged to shape your own curriculum in the light of the teachers' skills, the students' interests, and the resources of the particular community in which your school is located." Everything hinged on relationships and dialogue.

The "Citizenship Curriculum" begins with "The Basic Set of Questions":

1. *Why are we (teachers and students) in freedom schools?*
2. *What is the Freedom Movement?*
3. *What alternatives does the Freedom Movement offer us?*

These were questions to think about continually, to return to again and again. There was also "The Secondary Set of Questions":

1. *What does the majority culture have that we want?*
2. *What does the majority culture have that we don't want?*
3. *What do we have that we want to keep?*

Such questions were designed to provoke a sense of agency and power in students, to allow them to think for themselves and discover, in the process of thinking, their own skills, capacities, hopes, and aspirations. They already had the answers in their heads and their experiences, at least in part, and because there was no single, simple "right" answer to these questions, students would all have a piece in shaping the answers, exploring complexity through dialogue, back and forth, and continual questioning. There was no sense of people defined by their deficits, no cluck-clucking over the "at risk" student or the deviant community. As Paul Lauter and Florence Howe, two freedom school volunteers, wrote: "The hidden assumptions behind a reliance on discussion are, first, that talk—*saying the words*—is a necessary step for discovery of self and social identity. Further, the *public* discovery—saying the words in a group—might lead to action." (The freedom school curriculum was published in *Radical Teacher*, 40 [Fall 1991].)

Public participation and social responsibility in the classroom, respect for the decency and worth and promise of every human being, acquisition of knowledge and skill—all of this in place of submissiveness, fear, self-doubt, oppression. Students say the word and thereby *name* the world. Students change themselves, and they set the conditions to change society.

We are in search of a pedagogy of experience and participation, a pedagogy both situated in and stretching beyond itself, a critical pedagogy capable of questioning, rethinking, reimagining. We are looking for teaching that is alive and dynamic, teaching that helps students grapple with the question "Where is my place in the world?"

My younger brother, Rick, has taught English, humanities, and journalism at Berkeley High School since 1995. Rick was a classics major in college, and he came to teaching late—he had already been an organizer, an activist, a chef, and a lot else. I have spent time with him in his classes, I have observed him teaching, and I respect and admire him deeply—he really is quite an extraordinary teacher. But before I go any further, I must warn you of my biases, I must confess the possibility of distortion. I respect and admire Rick as a teacher, as I said, and I love him as a person and as a brother, and so the lens of my observations is necessarily rose-colored. I think of the purposeful and courageous way he has always lived his life, of the keen intelligence he applies to the daily obstacles he—like each of us—faces, and, most notably, of the deep well of humanity he draws upon to think through issues or challenges in his teaching or in his family or in the larger communities he engages. To fill out the dimensions of my bias, I have to note that whenever Rick hears me relate an anecdote about his classroom or describe what I take to be one of his emblematic teaching moments, he says, in effect, and usually much later and with characteristic modesty, "I really liked *your* story about me; it's so much better than what actually happened." We both laugh, me a little uncertainly.

The first impression I get walking into his classroom is that everyone—Rick and the students, and even me, the guest—is remarkably comfortable. There is none of the forced formality or obvious unease that is a feature of so many classrooms, neither the fierce tension nor the fear nor the ritualistic indifference that marks off so much of life in schools, especially, it seems, high schools. This classroom is an island of decency.

Rick is working at his computer, but he looks up and greets the students one by one as they saunter in. He might ask one person about an older brother recovering from knee surgery, and another about how her college essay is coming. Eventually, and seamlessly, class is under way, and it feels like a continuing conversation, temporarily interrupted when time ran out yesterday. "I used to panic, trying to get everything I had in mind done," he tells me. "But then I realized, there's always tomorrow."

There are big questions that animate Rick's teaching, questions he returns to again and again because they are generative, expansive, inexhaustible: What does it mean to be a human being? What does it mean to be educated? What does it mean to take responsibility for ourselves and others? The important thing, he says, is to "engage in activities that allow students to be recognized as subjects, actors in their own dramas, authors of their own stories, makers of their own worlds."

Rick has a clutter of books and papers and projects covering his table, but he tends to it steadily, and one senses an order to the thing. It reminds me of his work space at home. The kids, too, have tables to spread out their books, papers, projects, and everyone, it seems, is eating a meal or a snack at some point during class. "I've never understood why there are rules against eating in class," Rick says. "Teenagers are hungry all the time, so they want to eat all the time. The adult obsession with food-on-a-schedule is some kind of unexamined Puritan myth, and it's a recipe for disaster." His kids come into class, get settled, and start eating. "I can read and eat myself," Rick adds. "I can eat and think, eat and carry on a conversation. I, of course, don't want to eat every half hour, but they seem to. So, if it makes them happy, why not?"

Rick is the director of a small school within Berkeley High School called Communication, Arts, and Sciences, and he and his colleagues always find ways to explode the curriculum in the interest of encountering deeper questions. When the freshman curriculum called for Walt Whitman and *Leaves of Grass,* Rick naturally brought Langston Hughes's homage and echo to Whitman: "I too Sing America / I am the darker brother ..." The students were soon singing America from a kaleidoscope of vantage points, and before long they were into a project on race, combing history and literature, current events and journalism, anthropology, sociology, and more. Teachers brought in film, essay, short story, photography, and they messed with the received knowledge, the commonsense categories of race that fuel so much lunacy and oppression in America. They urged the kids to resist the narrowing of their lives into simple boxes of race, encouraging voyages. Students read, photographed, interviewed one another and family members, and each eventually wrote a poem that begins with a "poetry stem" that Rick provided:

> They asked me to write down my race
> And I think very seriously
> And consider writing down the truth
> And have my answer read ...

Their poems end with another supplied line—"But I stop and simply write down"—followed by the students' closing response. Here are a handful of examples of student work.

They ask me to write down my race
And I think very seriously
And consider writing down the truth
And have my answer read,

I have a brother, a sister, a mother, and a father,

I have *Turbo* magazine that I read every day so
that I can learn more about tuning cars

I have a Honda Prelude, Ferrari F-50, Ferrari
360 Modena, Toyota Supra, and a Chevrolet
Corvette C-12 posted on my wall.

I have teachers who teach me and help me put
More knowledge into my head

I have a favorite baseball team which I think are
Going to win the World Series they are the Atlanta
Braves.

I have respect for elders and my peers at school

I have enough confidence to know that I will
Finish school and become a very good automotive engineer

I have a house with a backyard and lawn
I have friends who are there for me whenever I need them

I have brown skin and short black hair
I have brown eyes
I have a passion for cars
I have talent for playing baseball and football

But I stop
And simply write down
"Salvadoreno."

They ask me to write down my race
And I think very seriously
And consider writing down the truth
And have my answer read,

But it makes it hard when you must
Put all the things that make you the person
That you are aside and settle for simply your
Outside appearance, your skin color.

I think to myself,
There is so much more to me than my
Skin color shows.
I have Scottish green and hillsides in me,
And Congolese dancing feet.
I've got Black Foot and Seminole in my hair and skin too.
I got chocolate kisses in my eyes
And my father's appreciation for life and happiness.
I got boys and toys,
And that nice curvy figure.

But I stop
And simply write down
African American.

They ask me to write down my race
And I think very seriously
And consider writing down the truth
And have my answer read,

How my ancestors slept, woke, and died laying
Track so that one day a train might pass.
How they looked across the bay toward the
Glowing city from the island of angels.
How they were ripped from the earth, their skin
Ripped from their flesh, their flesh ripped
From their bones by bombs.
How they looked from within the camps, the
Piss ridden horse stalls they were forced to
Call home, and wonder how the atrocities could continue

I think of this but I stop
And simply write down
Asian.

They ask me to write down my race
And I think very seriously
And consider writing down the truth
And have my answer read,

I am a Gypsy princess! My Dad is a Romanian Gypsy
My grandmother on his side was a flamenco dancer

My last name is Scottish
My family has a castle in Scotland

My dad has dark hair and eyes
I have blonde hair

I am Arabic,
My Jedu, or my grandfather on my mom's side
Came from Iraq to go to university here,
Her name is Yasmeen, like the Jasmine flower

My mom has dark hair and brown skin

I have German blood,
My great-grandmother came in a boat,
With five children to America

My grandmother is Native American, Apache
She spoke the language

When someone assumes my race,
They say I am white or Anglo

My grandfather has an Arabic accent,
Am I really white? No way, well...

Does it show that I am?
Will they know the truth?
I have blue eyes
Will they double look me when I give them my paper?
So many questions...

But I stop
And simply write
Biracial.

Rick's students are struggling with their place in the world, their own fullness, participation, and freedom straining against a commonplace—the barrier of racial categories and boxes. Rick's classroom is comfortable, as I've said, but it's not simply what his students would approvingly call "chill." He's invented something here with his students through determined hard work and focused intention. They have read about race and identity together—texts like *Caucasia; When I Was Puerto Rican; Coffee Will Make You Black*—and they are no strangers to discussion about their lives, their backgrounds, their futures. They have gone on all-day retreats where conversation is lively and extended, and they have read Studs Terkel and Anna Deavere Smith as they have learned to interview people—first one another, then family members, finally into the broader community—creating "oral history archives" and capturing a wide range of experiences, reflections, and interpretations. They are finding themselves as free people, as authors, thinkers, and citizens. They name the world, and they name themselves; they resist the delusional lens of race, and in the process they create for themselves a classroom that is a republic of many voices.

Rick doesn't allow student work to simply pass to his desk and then back to the student as if the only useful relationship is one-to-one with him, and the only motivation a grade in the gradebook. Projects are developed and refined, edited and reworked. Eventually, student work finds its way to the public domain and an enhanced life: a wall of poetry at the school entrance, a video or an e-zine or a journal of collected works.

One of the most interesting and sustained projects of student work has been the "Slang Dictionary"—first published in 2001, and with a new edition each year. "In spite of the efforts of dictionary makers to freeze language," Rick says, "language is always a dynamic, changing, exciting world—as exciting as the human cultures it represents." He and his students study language not to critique Standard English—"though I hate to hear people call it 'proper English,'" he says—but rather to think about their own thinking, their own ways of making and expressing meaning. They note, for example, that in their "slanguage" the largest group of words and expressions circles around the concept of friend, lover, or groups of friends: home, homey, G, OG, dude, cousin, folks, cliqua, set, nizzle, boo, whoady, blood, patna, peeps, crew, bro, money.

James Baldwin in "A Talk to Teachers," which appeared in the *Saturday Review* (December 21, 1963), describes this central paradox of education:

> *The purpose of education, finally, is to create in a person the ability to look at the world for himself, to make his own decisions, to say to himself this is black or this is white, to decide for himself whether*

*there is a God in heaven or not. To ask questions of the universe,
and then learn to live with those questions, is the way he achieves
his own identity. But no society is really anxious to have that kind
of person around. What societies really, ideally, want is a citizenry
which will simply obey the rules of society.*

There is nothing more refreshing—or more dangerous—
than a mind in argument with itself. A teacher can demonstrate
this, embody it, and encourage it in her students. One way of
proceeding as one teaches the content, for example, is to simultaneously teach the questioning of that content. This might
mean "teaching the conflict," as the educator and literary
scholar Gerald Graff calls it, teaching, for example, *The Adventures of Huckleberry Finn* and simultaneously teaching all the
struggles and controversies and criticisms surrounding the
book from the start—Does the story promote disrespect for the
law? Does it glorify ignorance? Is it unfit for young readers? Is it
racist? Teaching *Huckleberry Finn* along with history, critical literature, and other books as well, *Roots*, say, and *Beloved*, bristles
with pedagogical possibilities.

Teaching toward freedom certainly means creating curriculum that is grounded in reality, reading history, for example,
as an essentially human construction, with human beings as
the engines of history. Further, it means approaching every
text as a peer, not a consumer, an agnostic, not an acolyte. Students with minds of their own, a teacher also with a mind of her
own—this is a republic of many voices, a space where the
widest range of students can find both the familiar and the
strange, nourishment and challenge, a variety of things to engage and stretch them. This is where students can grapple with
the generative question Who in the world am I?

We teachers must insist on the freedom to think and say
what we please, and we resist being bullied both by the tri-
umphalist, the ascendant, the powerful, and by the orthodox
seemingly on our own side. We insist on independence. At the

same time, and paradoxically, we accept that we will, and we must, affiliate, identify with groups and causes, take positions.

I must try to convince my students, and you must try to convince yours, to look at the world for themselves, to make their own decisions. I must insist that each has a mind of his own, each can speak—and you as their teacher will be a living demonstration—with her own distinctive voice, talking back to power when necessary, trying to articulate the truth, deflating the authoritative claims clamoring to capture all the available space, searching for what is not known, what is forgotten.

When we are teaching people who have been deprived of a decent education, for example, the least we can do is to tell the truth as we see it. In poor communities in Chicago, students often have a clear-eyed view of what the powerful think of them—they see the condition of the buildings, the state of the materials, and they sense what is lost, missing, or withheld. Teachers can help them notice, too, that they've been denied something more: free thought, free choice, and free expression. They've been denied the right to question, the right to inquire about first things, and teachers can help students open the questions and begin the inquiry.

Loving our students requires us to help them nourish their own self-love and self-trust. If I hope to be a good teacher, I must defend my students, especially against myself. I will teach, then, not credulousness but critical awareness, not easy belief but skepticism, not blind faith but curiosity. I want no reverence for what I say; I want no disciples.

The luminous thinker, transgressive diva, and prolific writer bell hooks says that education can be the practice of freedom when we recognize the classroom as "a location of possibility," a place where we might demand of ourselves "an openness of mind and heart that allows us to face reality even as we collectively imagine ways to move beyond boundaries, to transgress." Teaching that invites questioning and boundary crossing, that enables curiosity and transgression, inquiry and going beyond.

This educative gesture, this teaching movement, is what hooks calls the practice of freedom.

In a lovely French documentary film called *To Be and to Have* (2003) we meet Georges Lopez, a middle-aged, one-room-schoolhouse teacher in rural France caring for a dozen or so youngsters who appear to range in age from five or six to about twelve. The film opens with a long, still shot of the empty classroom—chairs on desks, brightly painted pictures everywhere, plants, photographs, pencils and markers. It is the classroom at rest, and one anticipates a sudden explosion of youthful energy as the day begins. But the camera lingers. And then, without fanfare, a turtle steps out from beneath a bookshelf, and then another. We watch the two plod slowly across the floor in a ponderous point, counterpoint.

The dance of the turtles is a metaphor for Lopez's teaching: things are slow, nothing is hurried. In a world of instant everything, of moving sidewalks and staircases, of fast food and processed words, Lopez acknowledges that the growth of a human being takes time. There is time to become deeply involved, time to pursue projects, time to make and correct mistakes, and time to resolve the little conflicts that will always erupt in a group. There is little evidence of the characteristic superficial encounter and the hurried plan—minutes here, minutes there—the curriculum of "I know; you don't know." All five senses are engaged, big kids helping younger students, everyone with responsibilities, expectations, jobs, goals, and limits. There's a palpable feel of growth and change, an exhilaration that our classroom now is not as it was yesterday, nor as it will be tomorrow, and neither are the students or the teacher. They are on a voyage with no clear beginning and no end in sight.

In a second-grade classroom I visited recently in Chicago I saw a job chart, a cleanup chart, a free-time chart, and a chart of favorite books; a street map, a transit map, and several distinctly different world maps sharing space with student-made maps of the classroom, the neighborhood, and their own homes; a cooking area with a "juice bar" and colorful posters depicting "Noodles," "Chile," "Mushrooms," "Cheeses of the World," and "Natural Dyes"; each child's specific self-authored and handmade stamp, diary, dictionary, thesaurus, "tiny books," icon, math books, puzzles, and board games; puppets; blocks; a bowl of leaves; a sofa and a rug; two large tree stumps; and a bin of scrap wood. Like Lopez's classroom the environment felt rich and deep, inviting and potentially engaging. I was dazzled by all the little things I had never seen or thought of before—the idea of a self-selected icon for each child, a symbol such as a sun or a toothbrush, which appeared next to the child's name on the board, the cubby, and books and papers, struck me as a smart addition to early reading; all the personalized handmade books extending even these very young students' sense of themselves as creators and authors. But what impressed me most with this collection of artifacts wasn't this or that piece in particular. Rather I was struck by the sense that this learning space was the intentional design of a particular intelligence, that the architect of the environment had a purpose and a vision for her students and herself, and that her hopes, priorities, and commitments— moral, intellectual, social, individual—were evident in dazzling detail in her classroom.

In November 1999 my brother Rick read in an Oakland newspaper the obituary of a sixteen-year-old girl from India named Sitha Vemireddy. She had died of carbon monoxide poisoning, an apparent accident in her apartment two blocks from Berkeley High School. Rick was curious: Did his students know Sitha Vemireddy? Was she a student at Berkeley? Why were no family members mentioned?

He brought the obituary to school and asked if anyone else had seen it. Of course no one had—teenagers generally don't read the obituaries—but several were now as curious as he had been, and two of his journalism students, Megan Greenwell and Ileana Montauk, set out in search of Sitha Vemireddy, hoping to tell her story.

They discovered that she had been a student neither at

Berkeley nor at any other high school in the area, and so they pursued the story into the South Asian community. When Greenwell was rebuffed by the manager of a restaurant Vemireddy was thought to have worked at, her curiosity and determination ratcheted up. Within days the two students broke a story in the school paper that dominated California news for weeks: "Young Indian Immigrant Dies," ran the headline, and the subhead: "South Asian Community says 'Indentured.'" Two high school kids had blown the lid off a major smuggling ring involving women sold into servitude in India and brought to the United States illegally to serve as restaurant workers, laborers, and domestic servants.

This all began with simple curiosity about the world we live in. It was pursued with tenacity and courage. Connections were made to larger issues of work and law, morality and profit, the coerced and voluntary migration of peoples, immigration policy, the status of women, and it continues to grow and unfold: two prominent California businessmen were arrested and await trial, and a Hollywood production company bought rights to the story from Greenwell and Montauk. This last development led to more soul-searching, more reflection, and more complexity. The young reporters decided to send one-third of the money they had made from the sale of the story rights to Sitha Vemireddy's family in India, but in planning this, they decided that they couldn't simply mail a check for a large amount of money into an impoverished rural village without potentially violent consequences. This determination led them to contact the United Nations, which put them in contact with a nongovernment organization operating in the area that could help them. The learning continues.

Democratic education is characterized fundamentally by dialogue—the principal vehicle for discussion, deliberation, reconsideration, and transformation. In every dialogue there exists the possibility of mistakes and misperceptions, struggle and emotion, and also of growth and change. This is because authentic dialogue is an unrehearsed act of thinking out loud, and it is based on a recognition that thinking is in large part a social activity, impossible to achieve without the stimulation of other minds. Dialogue is a collaborative enterprise, a communal endeavor, a participatory event. In dialogue we speak with the possibility of being heard, of touching hearts and changing minds, and we listen with the possibility of altering the angle of our own regard. We begin with the serious intention of engaging others, but since we enter the realm of the flexible and the reciprocal, often even of the playful, we know that this journey will change us. Dialogue ignites our imaginations and pushes us further along.

Dialogue also creates community, even if the community formed is sometimes filled with contention and conflict. It can be the harbinger of disequilibrium, making the familiar strange, stirring new awarenesses, new empathy, new appreciation of the complex. We approach with conviction tempered by agnosticism, skepticism, doubt, a sense of the contingent. Our goal is not so much to successfully assert a point of view, but to transform and to be transformed. Our commitment is to question, engage, explore, pay attention, and to look more deeply, again and again. Through dialogue we discover the possibility of renaming, of achieving something new. No one can remain exactly the same. One finds a place in the world as a member of the community.

Authentic dialogue addresses a fundamental conflict in teaching—the conflict between the teacher who knows and the students who do not know—and points us toward synthesis. In dialogue the teacher becomes the student of her students, and the students become the teachers of their teacher. Lines are blurred, authority subverted, a new journey undertaken.

Dialogue is a democratic impulse, a participatory gesture based on faith in the capacity of each person; it is a responsive recognition of the claims of others, as well as a recognition of one's own incompleteness. One doesn't know everything, of course. One accepts the fallibility of all inquiry, especially one's own, the contingency of all knowledge, and a multiplicity of perspectives and interpretations. One might, if one tries, find that exciting and a cause for hope, not despair.

I look to the original freedom schools not as an act of nostalgia, not as a curiosity, but because they are an available example of teaching toward freedom, a site we can mine for lessons to power our teaching today. We can build a freedom practice of our own as we search out contemporary freedom schools, places where student experience is the starting point for thinking, where dialogue, inquiry, and self-activity lead to transformation of self and community. One such project is Detroit Summer, organized a decade ago by the activists Jimmy Boggs and Grace Lee Boggs. Jimmy has passed away, but Grace, now eighty-eight, continues to bring vision, inspiration, wisdom, and energy to the project.

The goal of Detroit Summer is to respirit, redefine, and rebuild Detroit from the ground up—to enhance community life through the grassroots efforts of ordinary citizens. In the first Detroit Summer brochure Grace Lee Boggs wrote: "Our concern is with how our city has been disintegrating socially, economically, politically, morally, and ethically." She and her colleagues were convinced that no company or industry could step in and solve their problems for them, and that it was up to them "to put our hearts, our imaginations, our minds, and our hands together to create a vision and project concrete programs for developing the kinds of local enterprises that will provide meaningful jobs and income for all citizens."

Detroit Summer brings together college students, high school students, and community residents in workshops and intergenerational dialogues to explore historical and theoretical questions, to set agendas and make plans for an ambitious program of work and activity, and, most important, to provide a place in the world for youth to enact their dreams. The organizers assert that the Detroit schools deprive students of many things, principally the right to think and to choose, and so they enact an explicitly different model of education, one based on knowledge, thought, critique, and choice. Everyone is an actor, an historical subject, not an object, and everyone asks questions about what troubles and excites them, everyone participates. The work of Detroit Summer involves research, outreach, investigation, and action. In the past, projects have included initiating a recycling program; rehabilitating housing; slam poets and hip-hoppers teaching poetry for social change; providing a healthful-foods co-op; painting murals to beautify and to create public space for community voices; transforming vacant lots into community gardens; and creating a bicycle workshop, Back Alley Bikes, which teaches neighborhood youth how to repair bikes that they can then keep as a means to travel in a city without adequate public transportation.

Detroit Summer opposes the top-down factory model of education with its passive, inert students and authoritative, fill-in-the-blanks teachers with a model of young people motivated to learn as they engage in solving the real problems of their lives and communities. It is a vital alternative to the world that they have been given.

Julia was sixteen when she went to check out Detroit Summer. She had loved school as a kid, and she'd been eager to start high school, to begin what she thought would be a real and substantive education. "Reading books was my passion," she said. "Just learning about new things got me excited."

But high school wasn't what she had anticipated. "Learning was completely lost in my school," she said. "It was all, 'Stand here...Go there...Line up!'" The list of don'ts and can'ts took up all the available space, and seemingly lifeless kids dragged around school—disillusioned, dull, disconnected.

At Detroit Summer she found more of what she had hoped for—sustained discussions about interesting things, from the structure of poetry to the reasons behind urban decline. "We talked and we read," she said, "and we also did things." That first summer she and other students cleared a vacant lot and planted a vegetable and flower garden.

Julia's younger sister Angela, twelve at the time, hung around and participated in many of the activities, but what fired her imagination most were the poetry workshops. Angela Jones has been a Detroit Summer regular for a decade, a college graduate now and Peace Corps volunteer in Peru. In her first book of poetry, a chapbook titled *Tattoo Trinity*, she describes her path. The following is an excerpt from the poem "Self-Portrait":

Sistah be riding her bike in Detroit
From the eves of Eight Mile
To the Gideon of Grand River
Detroit, D-Town, De Tois, of three
These streets are her trinity
8mile the father Livernois the son
& Grand River her holy ghost

. . .

See, Grand River ain't made
From asphalt or H2o
It's a concept conceived in the mind
It tries to bind history to the present
So we know that it's still relevant

So sistah be pedaling fast past the past
Carrying visions of it with her
To the next street, to fend off defeat
Remembering is her mobility
An added fourth to her trinity
And right at the starting line
Of her spiritual coast

Is 8mile the father Livernois the son
& Grand River her holy ghost

For Angela, Detroit Summer and the writing workshops became education as the practice of freedom.

* * *

Another example of a modern freedom school is the network of
literacy workshops organized by the brilliant community educator Hal Adams. Hal has organized workshops from Seattle to
Boston, but the ones I have seen are all in Chicago. He takes inspiration from an idea he attributes to the Italian revolutionary Antonio Gramsci: Every person is a philosopher. Workshops
begin with Hal introducing that germinal idea, and then pro-
voking a discussion about why it matters. Hal believes that
power and domination are maintained by more than the stick
and the gun: those who control ideas also control lives. If ordinary people can gain confidence in their own ideas, he believes,
if they can see themselves as actors and not merely objects to
be acted upon, they will have the means to challenge the control that others exercise over them.

Hal thinks that when ordinary people adopt the ideas of the
dominant and the powerful and reject their own thoughts and
experiences as less important, they limit the scope of their
imaginations and, therefore, their own possible actions. He
wants his students to start with their own experiences, to develop confidence in themselves and their own ideas, and then
to express those ideas publicly, allowing essential but over-
looked truths to become seeds for change.

One workshop of mothers meeting at 9:00 A.M. in a Chicago
public school began with participants writing about their experiences of that very morning. When they shared their writing, one woman read a piece about an abandoned building she
passed each day, and how it frightened her. In the conversation
that followed, it became clear that others shared her perspective, and soon several women were writing about "Abandoned
Buildings" and "A Dangerous World." What she had experienced
as personal and private turned out to be common, and in the
classes became public. Within months the women had re-
searched housing law, attended housing court, and received an
order condemning the property. Inspired, the women founded a

grassroots think tank to take on other abuses in the community. These women discovered that seemingly simple writing contains important meaning, and that working together, they could develop ideas and take action. To achieve liberation, Hal argues, it is necessary to think for oneself, to reach goals through one's own collective effort rather than an appeal to outside authority. Hal Adams insists that everyone should work for a better, more just world, and that those who do not see this are "illiterate," no matter what they can read.

We teachers stand on the side of our students. We create a space where their voices can be heard, their experiences affirmed, their lives valued, their humanity asserted, enacted. Students cannot enter schools as "objects"—thingified doohickeys and widgets—and emerge as "subjects"—self-determined, conscious meaning makers, thoughtful, caring, self-activated, and free. Where is my place in the world? Link arms—your place is not off to the side; come to the table, sit with the others. This is your hand. This is your reality. This is where we name the world and together achieve our humanity. The dialogue begins.

4. Lifting the Weight of the World
WHAT ARE MY CHOICES?

In the 2002 novel *The Cave*, José Saramago's bleak but oddly hopeful portrait of alienation and the contemporary world, Cipriano Algor, a sixty-four-year-old potter, lives in his small pottery with his pregnant daughter Marta and his son-in-law Marçal Gacho, a guard at the monolithic Center in the heart of the city, an hour away. Cipriano is informed by the Assistant Head of Department at the Center that pottery is no longer selling and that Cipriano's contracts will be canceled. Pottery breaks, Cipriano is told; plastic is more modern, more practical. Cipriano feels himself to be a man out of time, an anachronism. This bad news comes just as Marçal learns that he will be promoted to the post of resident guard with the added privilege of living in a small apartment at the Center. Cipriano resists the move for a time, but it is inevitable, and soon the family relocates.

The Center instructs new residents to bring nothing with them to their new home: "It is all there for you"—"arcades, shops, escalators, meeting points, cafes and restaurants . . . a carousel of horses, a carousel of space rockets, a center for toddlers, a center for the Third Age, a tunnel of love, a suspension bridge, a ghost train . . . a rifle range, a golf course, a giant map, a secret door... a wall of china, a taj mahal, an Egyptian pyramid, a temple of Karnak, a real aqueduct, a fjord, an Amazon river complete with Indians... a Trojan horse, an electric chair... a large dwarf, a small giant..." Everything about the environment urges people to consume and to be happy, to revel in the flashy carnival and to disconnect from any real engagement or accomplishment, to ask little, to feel nothing. Everyone seems to Cipriano to be anesthetized; he has the sensation of floating, weightless, in an illusory world.

Cipriano wanders, disoriented, feeling like a relic, until one day he arouses suspicion by knocking on a door. A guard comes out and tells Cipriano that there is nothing behind the door, that it simply "alerts us to who at the Center is curious." Cipriano is curious, and even more so now—something ominous seems at hand.

Late one night Cipriano follows Marçal to a subbasement where there had been much drilling and excavating. Inside a cave on a stone bench, he sees human skeletons fixed with metal spikes facing a wall—the diggers had apparently unearthed an archaeological treasure: Plato's Cave. "I don't want to continue living here," Cipriano announces. Cipriano, who had felt so out of place at the Center, suddenly sees his problem anew—his is the predicament of each of us: to be deceived into thinking that shadows and reflections and images are themselves reality, to be dazzled by forms removed from content, to be cut loose. Cipriano tells his daughter and son-in-law that he will not spend the rest of his days "tied to a stone bench staring at a wall," like all who surround him.

The whole family sets off, then, in a truck bound for the great unknown, as if on a river sweeping them along. Marçal tells the others that as he left the Center he saw a huge banner: COMING SOON, PUBLIC OPENING OF PLATO'S CAVE, AN EXCLUSIVE ATTRACTION ... BUY YOUR TICKET NOW. Everything a spectacle, and every spectacle packaged and for sale, nothing of substance or vitality or real significance. The family's odyssey is toward a world where they might participate more actively and live more fully, where they might once again be grounded in the earth and experience the realness of the world, where they might find their freedom.

I have tried to sketch here a pedagogy of hope and possibility, an approach to teaching toward freedom, which is, necessarily, a pedagogy of conflict and contention. I have portrayed teaching as a devotion to helping all human beings reach the full measure of their humanity, their enlightenment and liberation, resisting the persistent efforts to use schooling as an instrument of control or oppression. Teaching for humanization, I have argued, is a choice, and more likely to be made by those who face—clear-eyed and resolute—the obstacles before them, when they grasp, as well, the dimensions of what is at stake. We notice, then, that teaching is a site of hope and struggle, a contested space involving ideas about a future world we want to work toward and inhabit.

I have argued in favor of making our moral commitments explicit because these commitments operate at a different, more profound level and on a firmer base than, say, skills, or even dispositions of mind. Knowing where we stand, knowing what we stand for, we might negotiate the troubled waters of teaching and schooling more effectively and more faithfully.

For me, our foremost commitment must be to our students: We take their side. We take their side as learners, supporting their efforts to become wiser, more capable, more enlightened, and we take their side as citizens, encouraging their own specific and collective pathways toward freedom. We recognize and support their full humanity. We resist every attempt to degrade, diminish, or reduce them.

Our second commitment is to create a republic of many voices, an environment and a pedagogy that honors the humanity of each and that orchestrates a meeting place for all.

I turn now to another essential commitment—the tricky business of feeling the weight of the world. We already have one eye focused on our students and the other on ourselves. We have one eye on the physical environment and the other on the emotional and social and political spaces of teaching. Finally, we must not only see the world but we must feel the weight of it as we ask, What are my choices, and What are my chances?

The poet Jane Hirshfield argues that poetry can help you "find your way to a larger life than would otherwise be yours to live." That larger life is both interior and exterior, and it demands a traveling inward as well as an engagement outward. Traveling inward provokes the imagination, which lies at the heart of change. Without an imagination everything is simply there, lying still and flat on the surface, inert, static, immutable. A useful definition of "bigot" might be a person whose imagination has been wounded or killed. But with our imaginations intact and stimulated, the world we find is not so much a fact as a launching pad. Of course, imagination must be brought to life in contact with a world. Carlos Fuentes argues that all modern fiction is "a reflection of our presence in the world as problematic beings in an unending history, whose continuity depends on subjecting reality to the imagination." Hirshfield encourages moving inside, even as she rejects a kind of preoccupation with the self—"That is narcissism," she says, "not the path of wisdom." Balance is sought through wider encounters: "The weight of the world [is] only felt by your own lifting shoulders and arms," she says. The world is unrecognizable until it is touched, unknown until it is experienced. We apprehend the world—we see its scope and its borders and the choices it offers—and we understand our special place in it, only when we grab hold of it and try to lift it up.

In "Let America Be America Again" (in *The Collected Poems of Langston Hughes*, 1994), a wildly conflicted love poem to America, Langston Hughes describes the world as he sees it, as he encounters its barriers and limits, its barbed wire and its bars, as he feels the weight of it on his own lifting shoulders and arms. It begins this way:

Let America be America again.
Let it be the dream it used to be.
Let it be the pioneer on the plain
Seeking a home where he himself is free.

(America never was America to me.)

Let America be the dream the dreamers dreamed—
Let it be that great strong land of love
Where never kings connive nor tyrants scheme
That any man be crushed by one above.

(It never was America to me.)

O, let my land be a land where Liberty
Is crowned with no false patriotic wreath,
But opportunity is real, and life is free,
Equality is in the air we breathe.

(There's never been equality for me,
Nor freedom in this "homeland of the free.")

Hughes's imagination is both encumbered and enhanced by what has been called the social accusation of blackness in white America. Hughes chooses not to run from the indictment, but to take it on, to embrace it and thereby bend it toward his own humanistic purposes. He describes a world of walls and chains, and, simultaneously, he dreams a world of possibility, a world that could be but is not yet.

For me Langston Hughes is a bright and clarifying light reminding me that to be fully human, to be free, means to name the obstacles to your own fulfillment and freedom, the impediments to your own expansive humanity, to resist the forces bent on reducing you, categorizing you, turning you into a thing. The content of freedom is found in those public squares where people face one another authentically, where they come together to identify and overcome barriers. Those are the spaces where we find our own voices, our potential power, and our hope.

Unless we live in a perfect world—and the one thing I know in advance about the idea of a perfect world, about presumed utopias of any kind (and I've tried to live in more than one) is that I will never be satisfied there—then part of our work is the work of identifying the lions on the path to our own integrity. We don't necessarily know what to do but we do know that opportunities to choose for the good are everywhere. W. E. B. Du Bois said: "We must complain. Yes, plain, blunt complaint, ceaseless agitation, unfailing exposure of dishonesty and wrong—this is the ancient, unerring way to liberty, and we must follow it." When we see unjust suffering, unnecessary pain, undeserved hardship, we must complain—we can, at the very least, acknowledge, look, and listen. We can also insist on our right to remain skeptical in the face of credulousness, questioning of any of the true believers. Still, in a world so profoundly out of balance, each of us can find more than enough to do.

"All of life is a reprieve," the legal scholar Derrick Bell wrote in 2002, "a fact we acknowledge with reluctance." In his reflection on activism, *Ethical Ambition: Living a Life of Meaning and Worth*, Bell goes on to argue that we must search for satisfaction in the voyage, we must find our integrity in the struggle, because no matter how hard we work for justice we will never get there—"Perfection will evade us," he says. There is always more to do, and there always will be more to do.

Because there is more to do, I am drawn again and again to the activists: that ragged and fractious collection of outcasts, dreamers, eccentrics, romantics, and idealists. These are the people who name themselves in opposition, moving toward what they hope will be a better world; they define themselves by taking the weight of the world onto their shoulders, and by acting on what the known demands. My own imagination—my sense of the moral and the good—is nourished and challenged by those who break with the status quo and act for something more just, more fair, something new. "All's well," the town crier nightly assures the snug residents of the well-fortified city. But the activists' vocation is to remind us that all is not well—yes, friends, there is still more that must be done.

Activism is as vast as the human imagination, as deep as the human mind, as bold as the human heart, which, as the activist Dalia Sapon-Shevin, a young and brilliant ball of fire, points out, "is a muscle the size of your fist." Activism should not be confused with specific *tactics*; it is rather a particular *stance in the world*, one that draws attention to the need for repair. In the first place, activists act. They engage, participate, contribute, stand up, sit in, initiate, move—this is the signature characteristic. They question received wisdom, they wonder what could be but is not yet, and then they act. They open their eyes, identify injustices, and bring them to light so that they and others might see the truth of things more clearly, might feel the weight of them more fully. They dramatize a point or communicate a message, and they create a public space where people can come together authentically to create something new. They participate, then, in an expanding public busily becoming better informed, better educated. They take risks—not only when they break the law, but when they break with convention or the prevailing seductions of the tribe and the crowd. Sometimes they refuse to participate, and other times they participate in things forbidden to them, creating in that way the world they would like to live in.

Activists are all over the pages of history: the Boston Tea Party, the Minutemen confronting the British Army on Lexington Green, the Underground Railroad, the abolitionist John Brown at Harper's Ferry, Haymarket, the suffragettes, Flint, Selma, Atlantic City, Stonewall, Pine Ridge, Tierra Del Sur. Activists refused to participate when they burned draft cards or went to jail rather than serve in the armed forces during the American war against Vietnam, and when those who fought in Vietnam threw their medals at the White House in protest of what they now saw as an immoral enterprise. And activists participated in the officially prohibited when they created the world they imagined, integrating buses and public facilities in the segregated South, announcing through those acts that this was how they intended to live, black and white together. These were self-transforming acts for those who participated as well as world-transforming gestures for the larger community.

The civil rights movement set the moral agenda for a generation and became part of the landscape, part of the air people breathed—notions of freedom, liberation, social justice, and peace became more than abstractions, became in fact embodied and trembling and real, concrete things to enact and to live. Participatory democracy was something to breathe in and breathe out, something to experience in its dailiness, as was the cultural upheaval that followed. In all of this people thought of themselves as breaking through a range of imposed barriers to their full humanity, of dreaming beyond borders and then transgressing the boundaries of the given. Disinclined to petition power or to beg for an end to injustice, many acted as if they lived in the world they desired—we ought to be able to sit and eat peacefully at this lunch counter, and so we will do so; schools ought to be child-centered sites of liberation, and so we will build them—and in those actions helped to create the world of their imaginations. A large part of the border crossing involved a radical shift in consciousness, a rejection of both the conservative mainstream and the liberal reformers in favor of more fundamental structural and personal transformation. The world of choice opened up.

And the work goes on and on: street protests during World Trade Organization gatherings; antiwar mobilizations; teach-ins, blogs, and zines; Earth Liberation Front members sitting in trees to prevent destruction of the forests; tent cities on campuses dramatizing the plight of the child workers who produce college gear; members of the organization Critical Mass filling Lake Shore Drive in Chicago with bicycles, forcing cars off the road for the day, protesting our overdependence on automobiles; gay and lesbian couples and their supporters overflowing the hallways of the Massachusetts State House, or lining up at San Francisco's City Hall to get married in a massive celebration of civil disobedience; artists on the West Side of Chicago painting over tobacco and alcohol ads with urban hieroglyphics containing urgent public health messages. Mobilizing, dramatizing, refusing, insisting, engaging, risking. And sometimes, when we don't know what else to do, simply witnessing: in the earliest days of the AIDS crisis, before the virus was even identified and before a demand could be clearly articulated, activists created the stunningly beautiful and important Quilt Project. Like the Sanitary Squads in Albert Camus's *The Plague*, the Quilt Project said: Because we must do *something*, we will look and listen, pay attention, witness—mostly, we refuse to turn our backs on suffering.

But any claim for the righteousness of an act rests, finally, on the rightness of the claim—on acting against injustice and for something better. Dorothy Day, founder of the Catholic Worker Movement and an activist her whole life, said, "I'm working toward a world in which it would be easier for people to behave decently." Not perfectly, but better.

Activism thrusts us into the world of moral choice, but it has no value in itself. Nor does courage. Nor does drama, or resistance. Not even the proclaimed or obvious virtue of the actors has moral value in itself. Everything depends on the truth of the state of affairs exposed, described, opposed—does the action resist unjust hurt, unnecessary suffering, avoidable pain? Does the action embody or at least provide a space for change? Did it educate others? This last question is the standard by which activism is gauged: while there is no way to be certain in advance, it is nonetheless essential to raise in the aftermath: Did the action inform, illuminate, alter, or expand our collective consciousness? Did it educate both participants and witnesses? Did it build a broader community?

Activism, then, is at best a pedagogical event, and education and activism are connected. Activists try to teach; teachers open the possibilities of greater choice. Therese Quinn, a professor at the Art Institute in Chicago, has created with her students a dazzling series of posters linking teaching with activism. Each features a photo of a teacher/activist—Paulo Freire, Myles Horton, James Baldwin—and a powerful quote from their work, and each contains a bold invitation: "Be an activist / Be a teacher—Change the world . . ." Here is the quote they selected from Horton: "A good radical education . . . wouldn't be anything about methods or techniques: it would be loving people first . . . And that means all people everywhere, not just your family or your own countrymen or your own color. And wanting for them what you want for yourself. And then next is respect for people's abilities to learn and to act and to shape their own lives. You have to have confidence that people can do that. The third thing is valuing their experiences. You can't say respect people if you don't respect their experience." Quinn is recruiting artists for her program in art education, and she is tapping into something deeper than a job. For her, teaching is a calling to change the world.

In the immediate aftermath of the September 11, 2001, terror attacks there was an uncharacteristic openness and curiosity among many Americans, an impulse to grasp the magnitude of events, to feel the weight of them, but also to move beyond shock to understanding, the possibility of awakening—something huge had occurred, that was beyond doubt, but where had it come from and how did it balance on the scale of global horror? What kind of a world were we living in?

I was grateful then to be a teacher, because a teacher, whatever else, simply shows up, witnesses, creates a space. Teaching gave me somewhere to go, someplace to be, some people to talk and think with. I always tell my students that we must provide a safe space for ourselves in our seminars, spaces for inquiry, truth seeking, and soul searching. We should speak to one another with respect, I insist, with the hope of being heard and understood, and we should simultaneously listen to one another with the possibility of being moved or changed. In the weeks following the attacks, each of us feeling raw and aggrieved, I argued that we should strive even harder to be kinder, more caring, and we should surely allow multiple expressions of strong feeling, but we should resist as best we could any gesture toward self-righteousness, replacing it with compassion, generosity, and imagination. I asked my students to draw freehand maps of the world, and for each of them there were blank spaces almost everywhere—Northern Africa and Central Asia, the Balkans and the Middle East, the Persian Gulf and the Arab countries, mostly empty. In those vast empty spaces lay a breakdown of education, perhaps, a failure of teaching or a kind of enforced ignorance; maybe those empty spaces revealed a problem that accompanies the easy comfort of living in the lap of privilege. Who in the world are we? we wondered. Can we feel the weight of our world? What are our choices?

Americans are famous worldwide for having neither a sense of history nor a sense of geography. Who in the world are we? Where in the world are we? These questions provoke a vague sense of satisfaction or discomfort, depending on your turn of mind, but they remain, for most, indistinct. We are disoriented. A 2002 National Geographic Society survey of eighteen- to twenty-four-year-old Americans found that 87 percent couldn't find Iraq on a map, 69 percent couldn't find Great Britain, and 11 percent couldn't find the United States. In place of curiosity, study, analysis, or even an honest appraisal of gaps and confusions, we are offered marching bands and waving flags, slogans, sound bites, and public relations: "The world's only superpower," "The greatest nation on earth," "The land of freedom and democracy." I heard an American GI stationed in Iraq interviewed on the radio in late 2003: "We're proud of what we've done here," he said. "There's a lot more to do, but when we arrived there was nothing." He's referring to the Cradle of Civilization. Whatever else one might say about Iraq, "nothing" is decidedly off. Who and where are we? What's going on here? What are my choices?

* * *

We share as human beings what Hannah Arendt called the "negative solidarity" of knowing that at any moment the fate of the earth is in the hands of a few powerful—and dangerous—men, and we must do something. We have an urgent interest in agreements that would prohibit the use of weapons of mass destruction, of course, but also, since power is always corrosive and corrupting, and agreements depend on "good faith," which can be easily broken, an interest, as well, in a bit less concentrated power, a bit more balance, a little less unchecked unity. If power is corrupting, hyperpower is hypercorrupting.

The chaos, uncertainty, and danger of the present moment are further expressed in the shrinking of public life and the eclipse of a citizenry that acts as a politically engaged social force, aware and concerned to participate in the decisions that affect all human lives. The collapse of communism—with all its tyranny, horrors, and faults—removed the sharpest available critique of capitalism as well as a partial restraint against U.S. aggression, and has rallied private and selfish interests to a social vision that has only a tenuous link to traditional goals like equality, liberty, and fraternity. Absolutism and evangelical moralism replace dialogue and negotiation, empire abroad is linked to the shredding of civil liberties and the promotion of fear at home. Freedom itself is reduced to a matter of individual choice, without regard to social consequences. To be free is to buy. Consumerism and free-market theory as an ideology undermine citizenship in a fundamental sense—focus groups, market research, and public relations all bypass the political process, and elections, for example, become rituals whereby powerful minorities manipulate real majorities. And even then, sometimes, as in the presidential election in 2000, individuals step in and take matters into their own hands.

In this perilous and undemocratic world, this world of resurrected empire and spectacular inequality, those of us who live our comfortable lives in our small once-protected enclaves need to engage in the urgent work of seeking justice beyond our blinkered vistas, understanding the mechanics and tough realities of inequality, imagining a better world—not a perfect world, but a better one—and then finding ways to mobilize people to participate in political life toward that better world. No government in power encourages dissent, none relishes an activist, politically savvy citizenry. All authority prefers obedience and conformity, docility, dependence, consensus. Governments tend to deceive their own people, oppose initiative, courage, or anything that might smack of citizens with minds of their own. We tell ourselves that ours is a government of, by, and for the people, but is it on these dimensions so different?

We might, then, distinguish between the U.S. government and the American people, noting that as citizens our responsibility is to speak truth to power, to point to the contradictions as we identify and understand them, to resist the unjust and the overly powerful, and to demand that this government act for the good of all people. We are, if we wallow in our privilege and our certainty, cut off. The blank spaces of the globe leave us stranded. As citizens our task, now as before, is to wake up and connect, to see the world as it really is, to feel the weight of it— we mobilize ourselves to act in search of enlightenment and freedom and justice. As teachers we take one further step: we engage young people as they open their eyes, look around, see the world for themselves, and feel the weight of it with their own lifting arms. We do not turn away; we stand alongside them.

Mara Sapon-Shevin, a teacher in Syracuse, New York, and the mother of the activist Dalia Sapon-Shevin, has written a provocative and shimmering teacher-and-parent activity guide to the Peace Calendar published each year by the Syracuse Cultural Workers. The guide presents an organizing theme for each month—January: It Takes Courage to Speak Out; February: We Can Make Amends for Past Injustices; March: Drastic Situations Call for Dramatic Response. There are activities suggested for all kinds of classrooms, for young children, adults, and everyone in between: reflections, mural making, interviews, petitions, investigations, mobilizations, study.

In any culture defined by an ideology of materialist acquisition, happiness is tied to notions of wealth and success. The prevailing wisdom tells us that this is just the way things are: "Human nature is selfish"; "Human beings are motivated by self-interest"; "It's a dog-eat-dog world." Or so it seems. But we might pause here and note, as this prevailing wisdom becomes common sense, that there is nothing more dogmatic or insistent than "common sense"—common sense is only common, only obvious, to the initiated. Aristotle for one found the "common sense" of self-interest to be nonsensical. He argued that our human nature drives us to fulfill our unique capacity for excellence and for virtue. The good life is by no means one of material wealth or social and political power, but is rather shaped by the effort to become more fully human. For Aristotle the path to deeper, more realized humanness is an arduous one—one develops virtues by practicing them, exercising them, trying them out; one becomes brave by acting bravely; compassionate by acting compassionately.

Other thinkers, too, have expressed a view of human nature dramatically different from the wealth/success paradigm. For Martin Luther King Jr., for example, the leading human virtue was love—practical love, gritty, complex, and difficult love. Human fulfillment comes from loving others, he said, acting out of love for others, practicing love, promoting love and fulfillment in our fellow humans, even when it is most difficult to do. "It is not enough for us to talk about love," he said. "There is another side called justice. . . . Justice is love correcting that which revolts against love." What are my choices? Extending the space where justice and love are visible, accessible, and perceived as options.

Building the social conditions that make love possible, then, that make virtue and excellence more likely, became King's main task. No one can thrive during a genocide; no one can thrive at war; no one can thrive while starving. This is practical ethics—if you want to be good you are more likely to get there if you build a good society. Ethics and moral commitment, then, must include an engagement with the material conditions of life. That is, an ethics of *feeling* is inadequate; there must also be an ethics of *acting*; of building peace and justice, of feeding the hungry and healing the sick, of feeling the weight of the world. This kind of ethics asks us to reach beyond self-interest, beyond charity or service in search of new forms of associative living. We think in terms of reciprocity, solidarity, and sharing the joys and the difficulties and the wealth of life.

Joining with others is in part an exercise in reaching beyond the boundaries of home, neighborhood, state, or nation. For most Americans, particularly privileged Americans, some form of exile, some traveling outside the boundaries of the easy and the familiar, is an essential condition to freedom, to full membership in the human community, even if it wins you few hometown friends. Transgressing privilege, not being entirely at home in our homes, is a step toward humanizing ourselves, expanding our horizons, becoming moral.

The problems are huge, as always, and they seem too big; our ability to respond puny by comparison. I can't do everything, we hear ourselves saying, but can we do anything? Anything at all? Doing anything is where we might start.

The importance for teachers of teaching toward freedom lies in several directions. First, classrooms are porous places, and while we can indeed create distinct spaces and environments in schools and classrooms to display, embody, and enact our human and learning values, these spaces are never entirely dissociated or disconnected. The larger world cannot be relinquished; it will, in one or another way, assert itself. Controversy flows over the transom; we discover pieces of it everywhere. Students not only live and participate in a larger world, they will sooner or later face that world with full responsibility for it, whether they know it or not. Solutions to problems will be found or not, opportunities will be seized or lost, humanity will move forward or backward. For teachers, the point is to expand the space where choices can be made.

In 1999 one of my brother Rick's journalism students, Finnegan Hamill, heard a presentation at his church about a youth peace group in Kosovo. He made e-mail contact with a Kosavar teenager and they began a complex, continuous correspondence. Finnegan was following a tenet of Rick's teaching: the kings and queens, presidents and prime ministers are not the only and usually not really the best sources of information, and in journalism, whatever else you do, you should go to the base. Who built the Pyramids? he would ask his students. What does the stonemason know that the pharaoh does not?

When the Serbs swept across Kosovo, Finnegan was the only American journalist with an eyewitness source on the ground. He wrote reports for the student newspaper, and then took a series of his friend's e-mails and made a documentary for Youth Radio called *Letters from Kosovo,* not using his friend's real name in the report, since she was facing real and palpable danger. Finnegan felt the weight of the world; his efforts gave a human face to the victims of this war.

In the spring of 2002 a group of teachers at Chicago's Curie High School sent an open letter to the school board announcing that they planned as a group to refuse to administer a standardized test that they found "not in the best interests of our students." This was, for them, one test too many—they felt the weight of the world on their kids—and their planned disobedience was big news locally. Teachers from other schools took up the challenge and soon a public debate was under way about standards and the educational value of tests, and momentum began to build against this specific evaluative measure. Within months the board announced it would discontinue the test, but not before a wider effort to rethink the entire testing business had begun.

Sometimes students lead the way, and wide-awake teachers—students of their students—can learn a thing or two about courage and integrity. A group of college-bound kids at Whitney Young High School boycotted the SATs, claiming that the tests undermined any notion of a thoughtful or engaged education. This rebellion of the privileged against a system that they claimed hurt all students challenged their teachers to speak out publicly for or against the SATs, and for or against supporting the students' action.

Teachers and parents must be willing to act on behalf of our students and our children. We cannot simply accede when clouds are gathering, threatening them and us. I don't know how to change the world; and I don't know if our efforts are in vain. But I do know that change in small places can gesture toward larger transformations, and that changing a single mind can unleash a universe of possibilities. We must be willing, then, to act for small changes rather than waiting for some monumental movement when everything will fall into place.

The triumph of a fierce and relentless market fundamentalism is everywhere apparent, on the street, of course, but penetrating our homes as well, our families, our places of worship—our vaunted private lives—while forcing a reimagined and redefined public space, encompassing everything from health care to criminal justice, from waste management to elections, from safety to the distribution of water. In this bizarrely misshapen world, hierarchy rules, competition of every kind is always good, profit an undisputed virtue, efficiency and standardization a given, advertising a fine art, individual consumption the pinnacle of participation. The current iteration of the school wars mirrors all this—the marketeers are in full eruption, leading the retreat from the dream of a robust, diverse, and well-funded public educational system in the hands of the many (the reality includes, of course, significant exclusions) toward a system of private schools for the benefit of a few. The Edison schools are an egregious example—steeped in the rhetoric of freedom and the market, these proudly for-profit McSchools produce nothing and sell nothing, relying instead on a neat shell game whose chief accomplishment seems to be to transfer public monies to private hands under the banner of "free choice." The dismantling of mass education is under way.

In less than full-blown mode the skirmishes are widespread,

and so are the markers: vast resources directed to the simplistic task of sorting youngsters into camps of winners and losers; intolerant school cultures that reward obedience and conformity while punishing initiative and courage; a curriculum that is fragmented, alienating, and irrelevant; layers of supervision and regulation that reduce the role of the teacher to that of a clerk or a functionary, and constitute a dagger in the intellectual and ethical heart of teaching.

To question the tenets of the marketeers, to wonder if our schools, for example, or our children are being well served by any of this is the essential duty of a teacher who is committed to ethical action.

There is in fact a need to rethink in fundamental terms the whole purpose and larger meaning of school in light of the end of work as we know it. We witness massive displacement, with all manner of attendant pauperization and alienation. What will this mean for human survival or happiness and well-being for all? What are our choices? Schooling as job training and career preparation is an anachronism, and yet that reductive goal is preached repeatedly from the White House to the state house. Schools need to radically reconsider and restructure in a way that connects to the reality of the modern world. Martin Luther King Jr. had a sense of this forty years ago: "The work which improves the conditions of mankind, the work which extends knowledge and increases power and enriches literature and elevates thought is not done to secure a living. It is not the task of slaves, driven to their task either by the lash of a master or by animal necessities. It is the work of men who perform it for their own sake.... In a...society where want is abolished, work of this sort could be enormously increased."

While schools are established to re-create the norms and values of the larger society, they are also sites of contention, reflecting, for example, the dynamic motion of society and the long-term struggles and conflicts between democratic impulses and oppressive relationships. To justify or recommend a society's schools, one must be able to somehow warrant the society that those schools serve. The "failure" of black schools in apartheid South Africa was after all no failure at all. It fit at least some of the overarching needs and goals of South African society. However, South Africa's schools were also a key source of the liberation movement, the place where liberating ideas were learned and sometimes even practiced. The sustained struggle of South African militants arose from the schools, and schools were both site and seedbed for the liberation struggle.

A similar argument can be made here at home—the failure of some schools and some children in Chicago, for example, is not due to a failure of the system. That is, if one acknowledges (even tentatively) that our society, too, is one of privilege and oppression, inequality, class divisions, and racial and gender stratifications, then one might view the schools as a whole as doing an adequate job both of sorting youngsters for various roles in society and convincing them that they, and they alone, deserve their various privileges and failures. Indeed, sorting students—curtailing choices, narrowing options—may be the single most brutal accomplishment of some schools, even if it runs counter to the ideal of education as a process that opens possibilities, provides opportunities to challenge and change fate, and empowers people to control their own lives. Nowhere is this contradiction more visible than in the experience of poor and black children and youth in American schools.

The Greek poet Constantine Cavafy's "Waiting for the Barbarians" (in *The Complete Poems of Cavafy,* translated by Rae Dalven, 1976), one of my favorite poems, is written in the form of questions and answers, and it begins this way:

What are we waiting for, assembled in the forum?

The barbarians are due here today.

On and on, question after question, all day long: Why aren't the legislators legislating, the orators orating? And always the

same answer: Because the barbarians are coming today; everything hinges on the arrival of the barbarians. But, then, late in
the day, an abrupt change of tone and pace:

Why this sudden restlessness, this confusion?
(How serious people's faces have become.)
Why are the streets and squares emptying so rapidly,
everyone going home so lost in thought?

Because night has fallen and the barbarians have
not come.
And some who have just returned from the border say
there are no barbarians any longer.

And now, what's going to happen to us without barbarians?
They were, those people, a kind of solution.

Cavafy captures perfectly an element of the modern predicament, the sense of creating an identity in some important part
in counterpoint to a mysterious and vaguely threatening out-
sider. The subaltern, the marginal, the other is necessary to the
stability of the group. They are, those people, a kind of solution.

David Malouf's *Remembering Babylon* (1993), set in a nine-
teenth-century settler community clinging to the Queensland
coast of Australia, begins with three white children playing near
the border between town and swamp. Suddenly they see an ap-
parition, "a shape more like a watery, heat-struck mirage than
a thing of substance," and as it approaches, it becomes clear
that the shape is in fact a white man, but with the "mangy, half-
starved look of a black." This is Jemmy, cast ashore sixteen years
earlier and cared for by aborigines, a kind of paradox of a white
man, familiar but strange, at once white and black. Jemmy's arrival initiates the unraveling of the community, for if he is white,
the settlers ask, what, then, are we? It is "the mixture of mon-
strous strangeness and unwelcome likeness" that makes him

so troubling. Comfortable categories are disrupted, assumptions ripped open. The horror of not being certain in their narrow categorical beliefs besets the townspeople.

The Nobel laureate J. M. Coetzee explores the notion of society constructing some monster called "the other" in a 1980 novel that borrows its title from Cavafy's poem: *Waiting for the Barbarians*. Coetzee imagines a magistrate who runs the affairs of a small frontier settlement on the fringes of a great empire, and who exists for decades undisturbed, untroubled, unthinking, enjoying the petty privileges of his position. One day a certain Colonel Joll arrives from the Third Bureau. He is an intelligence and interrogation expert, a perfect instrument of empire, and everything begins to change for the sleepwalking magistrate.

One day over tea Colonel Joll explains how he will learn the intentions of the barbarians by questioning the few who hang around near the town: "First I get lies, you see—this is what happens—first lies, then pressure, then more lies, then more pressure, then the break, then more pressure, then the truth." Pain is truth in the logic of empire; all else is subject to doubt.

The magistrate doesn't particularly like Joll, but he wants to keep current with what's happening in his precincts. One night he decides to see for himself, but immediately regrets his choice: "I ought never to have taken my lantern to see what was going on in the hut by the granary. On the other hand, there was no way, once I had picked up the lantern, for me to put it down again."

The magistrate faces the truth of his situation—his unbearable complicity with a regime based on power and greed, not justice or decency. He soon realizes that "Spectacles of cruelty corrupt the hearts of the innocent," and he wishes he could go back to his innocence, living "outside the history that empire imposes."

Coetzee's tale is the story of all of us: complicit, but asleep. We worry that if we pick up the lantern, we won't be able to put it down. The Indian novelist Arundhati Roy, in the 2001 text

Power Politics, writes, "The trouble is that once you see it, you can't unsee it. And once you've seen it, keeping quiet, saying nothing becomes as political an act as speaking out. Either way, you're accountable." And implicated.

There are countless other obstacles to our being willing to pick up the lantern, to open our eyes, to stand up for the right or for the good—to feel the weight of the world and to choose to act for justice—and perhaps naming those obstacles can help us to overcome them.

One obstacle to feeling the weight of the world is the blindness of privilege. In an insightful essay that pivots on the problem of privilege and its obfuscations—that is, the problem of affluence and position and material wealth powerfully linked to anesthetized consciousness and the resultant spiritual and moral poverty—Paul Crowley from Lesley University evokes the image of Lady Bountiful with that irritating beneficent gleam in her eye as she happily delivers holiday food baskets to the ghetto slums of the poor, conveniently overlooking the social and political and economic forces that ensure her opulence and their destitution.

Privilege is not something the privileged have to embrace or even recognize in order to reap its benefits. I teach at a large university in the heart of Chicago, and my classes all meet at night to accommodate adult students who work. I was there for months before I registered what I had only vaguely noticed: male students quickly scattered for home after class, while women students gathered together in order to go in a group to the parking lot or the train. When I finally noticed and asked about it, it turned out to be orchestrated for a purpose—the women were banded together for safety. I and the other men had the privilege of leaving as we wanted, a privilege we never sought, but a privilege that was nonetheless ours without asking. We learned something, all of us, and we have consciously coordinated our after-class routines ever since.

A story in the morning newspaper—deep inside, buried between the noisy, unruly display ads—opened with this head: "Accused of Discrimination, Clothing Chain Settles Case." The story described a practice of "racial retailing"—store employees following black shoppers, and clerks refraining from inviting black customers to apply for store credit cards. While many of my white students—self-described as good and liberal—were amazed to hear of this injustice "so long after the victories of the civil rights movement," my African American students took the news with a kind of seething recognition, a familiarity that is at once knowing and outraged. Here we are again, they seemed to say, and, yes, here we are, face to face with American apartheid, a cruel and debasing separation and a hierarchy of racialized privilege and oppression with all its attendant self-justifications and mystifications. The structures of racial hierarchy are everywhere in evidence—changing forms from time to time, they are strictly enforced and remarkably consistent in substance—dragging the chains of an unresolved history along into each new year. And yet... and yet too many white people, sleeping the deep, deep American sleep, stubbornly insist on beginning each day as innocents.

Another obstacle to seeing the world and feeling its weight is the pull of the tribe. No one wants censure or sanction, and being a part of the dominant group is a constant seduction. No one wants to appear eccentric or weird, smug or superior. In all my acts against the American war in Vietnam, I think the hardest was standing in a crowd of colleagues and politely but firmly demanding that Vice President Hubert Humphrey explain his defense of the war. People thought I was being rude and impolite. I could feel embarrassment in every fiber of my being, and I could hear my mother's voice in my ear, berating me, reminding me that I had been raised better than this.

A young teacher I know who wants to eat lunch with his first-graders in the lunchroom has to walk a gauntlet of colleagues telling him that he's breaking with tradition and should come to the teachers' lunchroom, where the talk is mainly complaints about the kids, their families, and the administration. So far he has resisted, but he tells me that it's been tough for him.

Another obstacle to picking up the lantern is forgetting how the world could be better, or not attending to some vivid vision of a possible future. One evening my wife and I had the happy task of hosting a lively conversation in our living room with Justice Albie Sacks, a lifelong revolutionary, author of *The Soft Vengeance of a Freedom Fighter* (1999), and currently a justice on the Constitutional Court of South Africa, that nation's highest court. Albie embodies the wisdom of decades of struggle, and he also wears the wounds—he is missing an arm and an eye as the result of an assassination attempt years ago by the thuggish apartheid government.

There was much that was memorable about that conversation, but what stays with me most clearly is a point he made in dialogue with the historian and Palestinian activist Rashid Khalidi. During the antiapartheid struggle, Albie said, whenever he traveled abroad—to Europe or the United States—to raise funds or to build political support, he met with a similar reaction: Everyone understood perfectly the goal of destroying apartheid, the terrible injustice of the regime, the need to overthrow the evil and inhumane institution. What was more elusive, he said, more difficult for his audiences to comprehend and to accept, was the vision of a new transformed South Africa, something noble and special based on principles of democracy, of social and economic justice—"During that part of the talk I watched many eyes glaze over," he reported. The revolutionary as destroyer was easily grasped; the revolutionary as peaceful builder was harder to embrace. But, he went on, it was nonetheless essential that he push on and spend time on the vision and the dream, on expanding the arena of purposeful choice, the plan for a more decent future, because that conversation functioned as a kind of rudder for everything else. "If we knew and reminded ourselves regularly, if we *said the words*, if we elaborated and rethought where we were going," he said, "and if that effort was seen internally as every bit as essential as destroying the old regime, we had a better chance of avoiding the acts of in-humanity that are set to cut loose in any social upheaval, and of achieving, after all, what it was we were fighting for." Justice and dignity were the proper answer to apartheid.

In *Freedom Dreams: The Black Radical Imagination* (2002), Robin D. G. Kelley, arguing for the material importance of imagination and dreaming in any movement for social justice, makes the same point more succinctly: "Without new visions, we don't know what to build, only what to knock down." The power of narrative.

In spring 2001 a group of parents from Telpochcalli School in Chicago, frustrated by the lack of action on a verbal commitment to build a new high school in the overcrowded Little Village neighborhood, went to the site of the proposed school, pitched tents in what they now called Camp Caesar Chavez, and initiated a hunger strike. They had in their minds a vision of better educational choices for their kids, and they had a single demand for the superintendent: Come to this exact spot and meet with us about the proposed new school. Local parishes mobilized, the dream grew, and community residents began a vigil, but the superintendent refused to move—"We just don't have the money at this time," he said in interviews with the media. That summer the superintendent was pushed out of office by the mayor, and a new leader was appointed. His first official act was to announce that he had found money for the new high school, and a jubilant community celebrated. Many teachers in the neighborhood who had thought that the fight was mostly pie-in-the-sky were now welcomed into an enlarged alliance and an energized conversation about what the new school should do and be.

Another obstacle to seeing or taking the full measure of the world is what Norman Geras calls in the title of his 1998 book *The Contract of Mutual Indifference.* How to describe the modern predicament? How to understand the atrocities that have shaped the history of the last hundred years, the horrors that, while not different in kind or quality, are certainly distinct in terms of scale? "The contract of mutual indifference," the learned capacity to not see, to avert our eyes, to bury our heads in the sand, is perhaps a defining signature of our times, Geras argues. Saul Bellow had his fictional character Arthur Sammler note, "I know that human kind marks certain people for death. Against them there shuts a door." It's the shut doors, finally, that make the victimizing possible, and that intensify a sense of abandonment and victimization in the targets. The opposite of "moral," then, is not "immoral" so much as it is "indifferent." The normal world proceeds normally for the normal, and, the shut doors—that central act of immorality—mark our era.

The most devastating and memorable scene for me in *The Sorrow and the Pity*, Marcel Ophuls's 1971 documentary of France under Nazi occupation, takes place in a small town square near the German border. Ophuls is interviewing a mechanic who claims that no one knew about the atrocities of the holocaust. But, says Ophuls, the Jews were rounded up just here. True, says the mechanic, but we didn't know what was to happen. But, Ophuls interjects, they were herded into cattle cars right there. Yes, replies the mechanic, but we didn't know what was to happen. On and on and on... What do we need to know before we know? And before we act?

In February 2003 a group of students at Walter Payton High School announced to the media that they would walk out in protest of the impending war in Iraq and join a large demonstration in downtown Chicago. The principal immediately declared that any student who left the building would be suspended. Once again teachers were challenged to respond—if they followed the rules and reported students absent, the kids would be suspended; if they broke the rules, the kids might be okay, but they risked disciplinary action themselves. About fifty kids did walk out, and they marched miles to the main rally. Some teachers reported absences, some did not, but the debate about when the rules can or should be broken was fierce, now joined by parents and community members. The contract of mutual indifference was shredded.

Finally, an obstacle to lifting the weight of the world is the pull of credulousness, received wisdom, easy belief, certainty in an uncertain world. In *The Brothers Karamazov*, Dostoyevsky describes the human fear of freedom: "And men rejoice at being led like cattle again, with the terrible gift of freedom that brought them so much suffering removed from them." A tension lives between guarantees of happiness, peace of mind, and bread, and promises of freedom, which, according to the Grand Inquisitor, "men in their simplicity and their natural unruliness cannot even understand, which they fear and dread." All of us, I think, long for certainty in an uncertain world, something we can hold onto and believe in together—easy answers to our doubts, a single vaccine for the latest virus, the truth. We have difficulty tolerating anything as vague and enigmatic as freedom. The insistent message everywhere is accede, acquiesce, conform, play the game—you will be rewarded.

The Inquisitor points to rebels, whom he calls stupid people "rioting and driving out their teacher," people who will soon enough discover that they cannot keep up their rebellion—they will give it up and retreat into their own shared certainty. The iconoclasts will have their own icons, and the dogma of the rebels will be as insistent and totalizing as any other. The distractions and comforts and peace of mind that come from membership in a credulous community, then, replace the need for security police and barbed wire. We become entangled in our own doctrines and blinkered perceptions.

A teacher at liberal Evanston Township High School was censured for putting "oblique, indirect pressure on students" by wearing an antiwar button. She protested that others were wearing flags and yellow ribbons without comment, but to no avail. She was suspended and a group of students and parents rose up in her defense. And at Morton West High School yellow ribbons were distributed as a sign of support for American troops. The art teacher scalloped the bottom of the ribbon and taped it to a large NO WAR button. "I'm against the war," the teacher said, "but the troops include my students, who I love and want to see back here in school where they belong." The final project in her print-making class was this: "Take a position on the war and illustrate your position with a woodcut." Weeks later the front hall came alive with the colorful and spirited debate of the students' pieces. This teacher invited her students to engage beyond easy answers, to think, to feel, to wonder, to act.

Today talk of freedom is pervasive in every realm—free trade and the free world, free markets and free exchange—but it feels abstract; freedom seems a given that is both ubiquitous and distant, assumed but not available for active or concrete participation. Personal freedom—our self-proclaimed and celebrated rights and choices, our assumed autonomy and insistent independence—is similarly saturating but strangely off: free to drive anywhere, we find ourselves stuck in traffic; free to speak our minds, we don't have much to say; free to choose, we feel oddly entangled; free to vote for the candidate of our choice, we can't find anything distinctive about any of them. Most of us, of course, are also entirely dependent on others for a living; we have no voice and no vote in what will be produced or how.

Most of us experience the flattening and pacifying effects of a mass consumer society, the sense of being manipulated, lied to, shaped, and used by powerful forces. We hear all around us market fundamentalists promoting the idea that the purest forms of freedom and choice and democratic living can be easily reduced to a question of consumption. Many Americans behave as if freedom requires neither thought nor effort; we lucky few were somehow simply born free; it is our inherited state. We don't vote in large numbers, nor do we create or actively participate in public spaces. For all human beings, including us, there is the condition of being not entirely determined, but neither capable of absolute choice. No one chooses their parents or their historical moment; no one chooses a nation or tribe or religion to be born into. We are thrust into a world not of our choosing.

On the other hand each of us chooses who to be against that hard background of facts. In some situations we might accede, in others, refuse. Like everyone, we are situated; we are free. When freedom is abstractly and easily proclaimed, whether in school or in society, we do best, again, to proceed as skeptics.

In a society that claims a large and entirely settled notion of freedom as birthright, it is ironic to find so much human suffering and everyday misery at its heart. But this is precisely the American predicament: Massive, gaudy displays of our commodified freedom—the blaring brass bands, the smothering folds of flags waving lazily above us, the bombs bursting in air, thrilling, terrifying, suffocating, the insistent claims of a kind of fixed freedom that is simply there—become themselves obstacles to the accomplishment of authentic freedom. Certain that we are free, people abandon the search for freedom.

When freedom is posited as pageant, when our sense of it follows a script already written, we find ourselves reduced, unnerved, befuddled. The trappings of freedom, oddly, entangle us; they are themselves walls that must be breached in our search for freedom as an achievement of consciousness and action, freedom as a collective accomplishment to overcome what stands in the way of our humanity.

Freedom might be thought of as linked to the capacity to imagine a better world, linked as well to a coming together of many people to identify deficiencies and obstacles and the unendurable. Freedom, then, requires consciousness and collectivity and action. So much of the bewildering ennui of modern life is built upon our isolation from one another. We blame ourselves. After all, we are said to be free, we are told that we are a nation of communities, we see all around us the rigging and the decorations of democracy.

Still, the deep sense of alienation, of powerlessness, of a loss of any normal human agency abides, and an accompanying language of victimization and determinism takes hold. Overwhelmingly, there is a sense of helplessness, of stasis. Crime, crummy schools, unemployment—these are simply *there*, God-given and unchangeable. An attitude of alienation, abandonment, and atomization descends and permeates our relationships.

The enduring loneliness is propelled in some measure by the official insistence that democracy is a text already written—it is the flag; it is the vote. Never mind the Tweedledee-Tweedledum sameness of the Republicrats; never mind the millions of dollars required to hold office; never mind the alienation of most people from meaningful public life. Our democracy is good; your problems are personal.

To think of democracy as participatory, to think of people actually making the decisions that affect our lives, is to notice that while we experience our problems as personal—we can't find adequate child care, perhaps, or our child is not learning as she should in school, or the options for our aging parents are inadequate—they are, indeed, social. It is to move from me to us, from loneliness to society. It is to move in a different direction.

To be human is to live alone on the nerve islands of our bodies. To connect with another is to imagine with sympathy. The bridge of humanity is constructed on imagination, a certain kind of imagination, mediated by words. The brilliant Chicano poet Jimmy Santiago Baca, writing from prison, saw "Bridges of fire between me and everything I saw," and Walt Whitman wrote "I do not ask the wounded person how he feels, I become the wounded person." Whitman continues, "Whoever walks a furlong without sympathy, walks to his own funeral dressed in his shroud."

Justice asks for more than truth telling, more than forgiveness, but what? Reparations? Restitution? What more? One wonders how reconciliation will ever come. One feels the danger everywhere, heightened now by the suffocating, manufactured unanimity. Don't look. Don't hear. Don't speak.

In 1994 Illinois was scheduled to execute John Wayne Gacy, the children's-party clown and building contractor who over many years had raped, then tortured and murdered as many as thirty-three young men, burying their bodies under the basement of his home. I was both a teacher and a parent—our own boys were sixteen, thirteen, and thirteen that year. It was easy to invest in Gacy the wild, vast range of fears I had for kids and for my own boys' safe passage through adolescence. Everything threatened, it seemed, and Gacy could stand as the convenient embodiment of that threat.

But as the execution approached, something shifted. Perhaps it was the tone of reports on the radio, the giddy glee with which so many seemed to anticipate the state—which already had him bound and caged and harmless—killing this guy. In any case my wife, Bernardine, and I were having the same sick feelings, and we agreed that one of us should go and protest what was happening. So on the appointed date we had dinner with the kids, they set about their homework, and I drove down to Statesville with a little sign that said: "The State of Illinois Shalt Not Kill."

I got there an hour before the scheduled execution, and had to park a mile from the prison—the roads were jammed with people, mostly young, drinking beer, listening to rock on boom boxes, dancing, and cheering lustily with each radio announcement of the countdown. I felt even sicker as I made my sorry way to the front gate with my sign tucked discreetly under my arm.

When I arrived I was cheered to find that I wasn't entirely alone: nine nuns—each a teacher—holding candles stood in a shaky circle with Larry Marshall, a lawyer whose office is next to Bernardine's at Northwestern University, and his fiancée, the legal scholar Michelle Oberman. There we were, a dozen pilgrims standing in the dark surrounded by thousands of chanting celebrants. I often inhabit a marginal space, but that night, holding my little ragged sign, whistling in the wind, I was on the farthest fringe, feeling lonely.

Perhaps we were tilting at windmills that night, but something was already under way that would shake the criminal justice system in Illinois to its core. Larry Marshall was pressing the case of Rolando Cruz, a death-row inmate convicted of raping and murdering a young girl in suburban DuPage County. Cruz's retrial and acquittal opened a floodgate: over the next few years Marshall and his colleagues won case after case of death-row inmates who had been wrongfully convicted.

The *Chicago Tribune* published a scathing investigative series on capital crimes, and it became clear that the system was broken: since 1977, of the 270 plus people condemned in Illinois, 12 had been executed, 13 exonerated, and about 90 had their death sentences reversed on appeal and received a lesser sentence the second time around.

The people of Illinois may be "pro–death penalty," but that doesn't mean they favor randomly killing innocent people. On his last day in office in January 2003, Governor George Ryan, a lifelong Republican politico engulfed in scandal, commuted the sentences of all 167 death row inmates, pardoning several. Over the course of a long, tormented journey, Ryan had become a student who had looked into the face of the death system and recoiled—he became an abolitionist, in no small measure because of the efforts of his teacher, Larry Marshall.

I remember that dark night almost a decade past standing outside the gates at Statesville with our tiny candles. That's all I'd done, but I'm glad I was there, happy to have stood with Larry, a teacher whose work saved lives and changed the course of history. I didn't change the world, but I was changed by choosing to go. That, too, is part of the point.

Langston Hughes ends his love poem to America this way:

> A dream—
> Still beckoning to me!
>
> O, let America be America again—
> The land that never has been yet—
> And yet must be—
> The land where every man is free.

The land that's mine—
The poor man's, Indian's, Negro's ME—
Who made America,
Whose sweat and blood, whose faith and pain,
Whose hand at the foundry, whose plow in the rain,
Must bring back our mighty dream again.
From those who live like leeches on the people's lives,
We must take back our land again,
America!

O, yes,
I say it plain,
America never was America to me,
And yet I swear this oath—
America will be!
An ever-living seed,
Its dream
Lies deep in the heart of me.

We, the people, must redeem
Our land, the mines, the plants, the rivers,
The mountains and the endless plain—
All, all the stretch of these great green states—
And make America again!

Langston Hughes knew that America was both reality and idea, and he challenged himself as he challenges us to unite the two. He imagined himself beyond confinement. The young spiritual activist Eboo Patel has called America a "trauma of contradictions," a story still not fully written. When I was nineteen I joined a student organization whose founding document began, "We are people of this generation, bred in at least modest comfort...looking uneasily at the world we inherit." The challenge for today, then, is not unfamiliar, but it is unique in time and place—the American story must be rewritten again, right now, by this generation. It is the challenge to claim a tradition by adding your voice and experience to it. James Baldwin said, "I am not a ward of America. I'm one of the first Americans. I've earned a place at the table." So have we. So have the young. There are choices to be made, choices that will shape the lives we live, will make us worthy of the tradition or not. America is far from paradise, but here in America we can create spaces for a new world to be imagined and fought for.

In a prison letter to a friend, the German socialist Rosa Luxemburg said this about leading both an activist and a balanced life: "Then see to it that you remain a *Mensch*!" She continued: "Being a *Mensch* means happily throwing one's life 'on fate's great scale' if necessary, but, at the same time, enjoying every bright day and every beautiful cloud." She is urging her friend to feel the weight of the world alongside its beauty and its hopefulness.

Our commitment, then, is to open our eyes to the world, to the possible and the hopeful. What are my choices? To look and to see, to stand up and be counted, to dream, to listen, to accept disequilibrium, to act, to doubt, and to act again. And to stand *with* my students as they see and begin to feel the weight of the world for themselves.

5. Teaching toward Freedom

José Saramago, whose large allegorical novels set off aspects of the modern predicament in sharp relief, has served as itinerant philosopher and guide throughout these pages, so it seems only fitting to turn to him once more as our journey nears an end. Saramago's 1995 novel *The Stone Raft* opens as the Iberian Peninsula, without warning or explanation, breaks free of Europe and begins to drift slowly out to sea. The peninsula migrates east, stops, spins suddenly, and heads south, a float adrift on an unknown expanse of blue. "You can see where the crack originates," says the narrator, "but no one knows where it ends, just like life itself."

Five strangers are thrust together through an odd set of circumstances, and soon they set off on a voyage of their own. "Don't worry about things making sense," one says. "A journey only makes sense if you finish it, and we're still only half way there, or perhaps only at the beginning, who knows, until your journey on earth has ended I cannot tell you its meaning."

Our journey in this book has been a search for the ethical in teaching, and particularly for a set of moral commitments that might act as sextant and rudder in our own endless expanse of blue, the stormy seas that we will necessarily be called upon to navigate. I have mapped a pedagogy of potential and power, a terrain unsettled and unsettling, resisted and contested; I have argued that teaching at its best is an enterprise devoted to enlightenment and freedom, to the cause of humanity itself, and that teachers are often caught between that romantic-sounding ideal and the grubby business of domination and coercion which is the hallmark of so much that we call schooling. Teaching for humanization is hard, tough work, and it is more likely to be chosen by teachers who are wide awake to the true dimensions of the struggle. We note that education is always a site of hope as well as of conflict, and that the seemingly petty quarreling that marks life in classrooms and schools is often a proxy masking deeper, principled differences about what the future might be, and what it means to be human.

I have advocated for recognizing and supporting our students as a foremost moral commitment. We act sometimes as mentor and guide, sometimes as ally or merely witness, always as student of our students. We do not exploit or humiliate them; we resist especially the institutional workings that reduce or erase them, for we are on their side. We create in our classrooms an understanding of the inestimable, irreducible value of each human life, and a sense that each has the unique capacity to choose, to shape, and in concert with others to create reality.

We commit, as well, to creating a republic of many voices, an environment for learning characterized by dialogue, a place where every student can come forward as they really are, without masks, where every person can be both seen and heard, honored and respected. We create a space to enact an education linked to the lived lives of students and connected to a larger, dynamic world.

With one eye on our students and another on ourselves, we attend to both the learning environment and the concentric circles of context in which our teaching is enacted. We commit to striving for true awareness of the larger world, to feeling the weight of it as we attempt to lift it up.

This is the substance of teaching toward freedom—it indicates a direction, but it is not an easily defined or definitive destination. Teaching toward freedom is never settled, never finished, but is, rather, a stance and a commitment in the world. We commit to the journey, and in that gesture we must learn to resist orthodoxy, to open up to the new and to the possible even as we reign in the extravagant and the metaphysical. This creates a full circle: if we imagine each of our students as an unruly spark of meaning-making energy on a voyage of discovery and surprise, how can we imagine ourselves as anything less? Since energy is nothing but the potential for change—if my students have it, why wouldn't I have it as well? Each of my students is a work in progress, and I need to see that I, too, am unfinished, dynamic, in transit and in motion. I, too, am a node of energy able, perhaps even eager, to change. I, too, am a work in progress.

José Saramago's stone raft is, of course, also the planet earth, gliding through the fathomless blue, turning and turning around a rather small and insignificant star, charted and yet not, fated but free, so large that none of us feels exactly like a sailor, so small that we tremble at our insignificance. There are so many gigantic things lying outside our control, so much that seems to just happen to us, it can be difficult at times to take hold of our power and our agency, to make something of it.

"So often we need a whole lifetime in order to change," Saramago writes. "We think a great deal, weigh things up and vacillate, then we go back to the beginning, we think and think, we displace ourselves on the tracks of time with a circular movement, like those clouds of dust, dead leaves, debris, that have no strength for anything more, better by far that we should live in a land of hurricanes."

For better or for worse, we do indeed live in a land of hurricanes, and we ride the crest of a zephyr. Paradoxically, and a little disquietingly, it is also a land disguised as calm, and we too often experience ourselves as little more than dead leaves and debris.

We need to learn to ask questions of ourselves and of others, to ask risky questions and baffling questions, dynamic questions, and then to live within them, within the contingent answers and the tentative conclusions and the deeper, more disturbing questions that lie just beneath.

Even when we think of ourselves as open-minded, we are in some large part prisoners of constrained definitions of society, narrow conceptions of human capability. We accept too much. Perhaps the hardest lesson for all of us to learn is that human identity is not settled but in motion, that reality is not fixed and solid but dynamic. We too often act as if the future is going to be a lot like the present, only more so, but the truth is that the future is unknown, of course, and also unknowable. Think of any decade in the twentieth century, and the opening years of the twenty-first century . . . no one could have predicted the changes just ahead, and the impact of those changes on so many aspects of our lives. The atomic bomb. AIDS. Personal computers and the World Wide Web. Rosa Parks. Hip-hop. Reality TV. McDonald's. Starbucks. DVDs. Genocide in Cambodia, Rwanda, and Bosnia. September 11. Knowing this, it is obviously foolish to imagine the future as the present *plus*, now in spades, and yet our imaginations so often fail us.

We might, then, cultivate as an article of faith the belief that every human being can exceed where they are now, each is capable of surpassing him or herself, of going beyond. One of our challenges, then, is to live and work in the belief that *we ourselves, along with our students, can do what's never been done*, and we might—you can change your life, you can rock your world. Another is to look down the road, and take responsibility for what's coming. What could the world look like in 2050? What am I doing to make it so? Remember: you can change your life, you can change your world. What would you do if you were president of the United States? And, incidentally, why couldn't you be? You're a citizen. Go ahead. Be the president. In a wonderfully whimsical piece written for In These Times (June 20, 2003), the actor Woody Harrelson responds to a London cabdriver who asks him what he would do in President George W. Bush's shoes. "Easy," he answers. "I'd honor Kyoto. Join the world court. I'd stop subsidizing earth rapers like Monsanto, Dupont and Exxon. I'd shut down the nuclear power plants. So I already have two hundred billion saved from corporate welfare. I'd save another one hundred billion by stopping the war on noncorporate drugs. And I'd cut the defense budget in half so they'd have to get by on a measly two hundred billion a year. I've already saved half a trillion bucks by saying no to polluters and warmongers. Then I'd give three hundred billion back to the taxpayers. I'd take the rest and pay the people teaching our children what they deserve. I'd put one hundred billion into alternative fuels and renewable energy. I'd revive the Chemurgy movement, which made the farmer the root of the economy, and make paper and fuel from wheat straw, rice straw and hemp. Not only would I attend, I'd sponsor the next Earth Summit. And, of course, I'd give myself a fat raise." *Pay the people teaching our children.* The man has brains.

Carl Sandberg describes a powerful ruler—a raja or an emperor in a land far away and long, long ago—who, for all his wealth and position, was constantly ill at ease. He agonized over the meaning of life. He just couldn't seem to nail down the point of it all, and so one day he called together the greatest teachers and prophets and philosophers, and he commanded them to deliberate, discuss, debate, and finally to sum up all that was known and believed about human life. After long, sometimes torturous and contentious consideration, they offered three words in sequence: Born...Troubles...Died. When the ruler sent them back, asking now for a single word, the wise ones came to this: *Maybe.* Langston Hughes expressed something similar in a playful way: "Birthins' hard/Dyins' mean/Get some lovin' in between."

"If I only had a home...a heart...a brain...the nerve." The four hopeful seekers skipping together down the yellow brick road toward Oz sing their desires to one another and to the heavens. Each has diagnosed a deficiency, identified a lack, recognized a need. Each has become painfully conscious of something missing, a hole in need of repair. Each is stirred to action against an obstacle to his or her fullness, and each gathers momentum and power from the others, from intimate relationship forged through collective struggle.

This is not a bad start for teachers seeking a vocabulary of basics in their quest for wholeness and for goodness in teaching—a home, a heart, a brain, the nerve. There is more, to be sure, but these can send you skipping down your own yellow brick road into the beyond.

Teaching is intellectual and ethical work; it takes a thoughtful, reflective, and caring person to do it well. It takes a brain and a heart. The first and fundamental challenge for teachers is to embrace students as three-dimensional creatures, as distinct human beings with hearts and minds and skills and dreams and capacities of their own, as people much like ourselves. This embrace is initially an act of faith—we must assume capacity even when it is not immediately available or visible—because we work most often in schools where aggregating and grouping kids on the flimsiest evidence is considered common sense, where the toxic habit of labeling youngsters on the basis of their deficits is a commonplace. A teacher needs a brain to break through the cotton wool smothering the mind, to see beyond the blizzard of labels to this specific child, trembling and whole and real, and to this one, and to this. And a teacher needs a heart to fully grasp the importance of that gesture, to recognize in the deepest core of your being that every child is precious, each unduplicable, the one and only who will ever trod this earth, deserving of the best a teacher can give—respect, awe, reverence, commitment.

A teacher who takes up this fundamental challenge is a teacher working against the grain—you have got to have the nerve. All the pressures of schooling push teachers to act as clerks and functionaries—interchangeable parts in a vast and gleaming and highly rationalized production line. To teach with a heart and a brain—to see education as a deeply humanizing enterprise, to teach toward freedom, toward opening infinite possibilities for your students—requires courage. Courage is a quality nurtured in solidarity with others—it is an achievement of colleagues and allies. In order to teach with thought and care and courage, you really need a home.

The four seekers lurching toward Oz provide another lesson for us. We can all constantly work to identify obstacles to our freedom, to our fullness. The obstacles will change as we develop and grow, but there is always more to know, always more to become, more to do. In our quest we can all reach out for allies and friends to give us strength and power and courage to move on. And we can now know in advance that there is no wizard at the end of the road, no higher power with a magic wand to solve our all-too-human problems. Recognizing that the people with the problems are also the people with the solutions, and that waiting for the lawmakers, the system, or the union— or any other fraudulent great power hidden behind a heavy curtain—to save us or to get it right before we get it right is to wait a lifetime. We can look inside ourselves, summon strengths we never knew we had, connect up with other teachers and parents and kids to create the schools and classrooms we deserve— thoughtful places of decency, sites of peace and freedom and justice. We are on the way, then, to our real Emerald Cities.

Stanley Kunitz, former poet laureate of the United States, wrote in the introduction to his collection *Passing Through: The Later Poems New and Selected* (1997): "Poets are not easily domesticated . . . and they can be outrageous; but they are also idealists and visionaries whose presence is needed . . . to clear the air of corruption and hypocrisy, to mock oppression, and to challenge [spiritual] apathy." To clear the air of corruption and hypocrisy, to mock oppression, to challenge apathy—poets, yes, by all means, and also teachers and citizens, students and activists.

Idealism in this sense is neither a synonym for naïveté nor for the superstitious and willful abandonment of reality—the poet/teacher/student is always leaning forward, on a quest for knowledge, enlightenment, ultimately for the truth. If our destiny is to fall short—if enlightenment is always partial, and truth, in an ultimate sense, always elusive—that in no way diminishes the importance of our attempt. We search for truth as an ethical imperative, a moral stance, and a guide to integrity.

Further, our stance allows us to unstick ourselves from some fictionalized past when everything was putatively perfect—the golden age in education, for example, when every schoolchild knew whose face had launched a thousand ships. The gold becomes dross, anyway, when we think of the class and race qualifications that once defined "every schoolchild." We unstick ourselves as well from a fixed, deterministic fantasy future when every conflict will be resolved, every synthesis achieved, every mystery explained.

This kind of idealism-in-tension is pulled between the cold, new world of the present, and a possible future, more peaceful, more just, more in balance than anything we have ever known. Idealists must be willing to live within this tension, one foot planted in the mud and muck of the world as we find it, the other striving toward a world that could be. We toil in fields not entirely of our making; we plant seeds for harvests we can only begin to imagine.

In *Galileo*, Bertolt Brecht brings some of the tensions between the various constructions of idealism to life. Galileo's breathtaking discoveries about the movement of the planets and the stars ignite in him the desire to pursue a particularly radical idealism: "The cities are narrow and so are the brains," he declares boldly. "Superstition and plague. But now the word is: since it is so, it does not remain so. For everything moves, my friend." With this, Galileo launches a revolution—it is his idealism against the idealism of the Church that must, in time, condemn the radical for challenging their privileged and dominant orthodoxy.

Galileo seems at first unstoppable: "It was always said that the stars were fastened to a crystal vault so they could not fall," he says. "Now we have taken heart and let them float in the air, without support, they are embarked on a great voyage—like us, who are also without support and embarked on a great voyage."

Here Galileo ups the ante. He questions the common sense, and he challenges the establishment in the realm of its own authority. For the Church, after all, the great voyage we are on cannot be thought of as occurring without support. It is, in fact, the opposite: a sanctioned and planned voyage, the steps entirely mapped out with clockwork precision and mathematical certainty, all the support we need in the institution of the Church itself.

Clearly more than theories of astronomy are in play here. The ideas, surely, but also the joy, the excitement, the reckless hope, all mark Galileo as a radical and an activist. After all, he could have just written a book, as Copernicus did, and let it go at that. But Galileo raised the stakes as high as he could: he wanted to teach the world, he wanted to make a revolution.

Galileo's struggle is punctuated with joy and grief, hope and despair, pain and torment and pressure, but when he finally capitulates and denounces *what he knows to be true*, when he betrays his fire to learn and to teach and is received by the Church back "into the ranks of the faithful," he is exiled from humanity—by his own words. In the end, he is confronted by a former student, one of his crestfallen disciples: "Many on all sides followed you with their eyes and ears," he says, "believing that you stood, not only for a particular view of the movement of the stars, but even more for the liberty of teaching—in all fields. Not then for any particular thoughts, but for the right to think at all. Which is in dispute." The right to think at all—a right that is in deep dispute in our schools, now, and in our society.

Martin Luther King Jr. famously said that the arc of the moral universe is long, but that it bends toward justice. This is not a scientific conclusion or an established fact, but rather an inspired expression of hope for a world that could be, but is not yet, a world that requires all of us to imagine and to act on behalf of freedom and enlightenment. It is a hope for humanity itself.

I am writing this early in the morning on the seventy-fifth anniversary of the birth of Martin Luther King Jr., and I'm filled with memories, surrounded by images, bombarded with announcements of the official sanitized remembrances scheduled for the national holiday in a few days. It is hard to believe that King never reached his fortieth year, that like Malcolm X he was assassinated at thirty-nine, and that he had been an activist for only thirteen years. But it's true: he was here, and then, suddenly, gone. Why, then, is he so central a part of the American imagination? What is the meaning of King's life and the legacy of his struggles?

It is immediately apparent that there is not a single, stable Martin Luther King Jr., solid, sanctified, and the same for all. Rather, there are several competing Kings, each dynamic and still alive; the King one chooses and claims, the King one embraces speaks to the challenges ahead even more than to the ones already past.

There is in the first place the revered national hero, the Martin Luther King Jr. of the propulsive and brilliant "I Have a Dream" speech at the Lincoln Memorial in 1963, the nonviolent apostle of *agape* who won the Nobel Peace Prize and brought about a benevolent revolution in race relations. The canonized King instructs us to love one another and to embrace our common humanity—his modern promoters tell us that huge progress has been made, that we are living in a postrevolutionary world where, as far as race in America is concerned, the problems and contradictions were all taken care of in the deep past. This King won, and in the wake of the Civil Rights and Voting Rights Acts went into a kind of early retirement.

The official version has too many blank spaces for me, and there is naturally another, more complicated and insurgent King who can also teach us a lot. The young, forceful preacher who led the protests in Montgomery, Birmingham, and Selma, and achieved an international following as a relentless warrior for freedom, continued to grow, to learn, and to fight long after the legal system of racial segregation was smashed. Unlike the mythic, iconic King, this one is considerably tougher to embrace by the powerful and the comfortable. This King saw life as a protracted struggle for freedom, with humanity ceaselessly confronting new and more complex obstacles requiring action and reflection, doubt and suffering, energy and affirmation and struggle. This King would not condemn the rioters in the ghetto before naming "the greatest purveyor of violence in the world today, my own government." This King was a teacher and a student, a tormented pilgrim, adrift in a world gone mad. This King was a work in progress to his last breath.

In 1967 King wrote, "For years I labored with the idea of reforming the existing institutions of society, a little change here, a little change there. Now I feel quite differently. I think you've got to have a reconstruction of the entire society, a revolution of values." This would be his theme for the final years of his life—the need for a radical revolution in values and a radical remaking of society.

King sought a revolution that would transform our "thing-oriented" society into a "person-oriented" community: "When machines and computers, profit motives and property rights are considered more important than people," he said, "the giant triplets of racism, militarism, and materialism are incapable of being conquered." He worried that technology without morality was a looming catastrophe: "Enlarged material powers spell enlarged peril if there is no proportionate growth of the soul." He warned of the danger of a country that had guided missiles in the hands of "misguided men."

King came to Chicago in 1967 to open a new front in his long, continuing fight for justice—no longer against de jure southern style racism, the fight would be against containment and control, for a revitalized and just society. King was determined to "break the system in Chicago," reasoning that if this solid bastion could be breached, the struggle would spread everywhere. He knew that the stakes were higher than anything he had undertaken before, and that the demands being worked out in Chicago would be fiercely resisted because they promised to "cost the nation something." King thought that the great struggles and sacrifices that had led to the well-known victories—Supreme Court rulings, federal legislation—were merely prelude. Those victories required no renouncing of privilege, no fundamental adjustments in wealth and power. In this sense they were bought on the cheap. What was needed was a profound reimagining and respiriting and readjusting—a radical revolution in values, a radical remaking of society.

Martin Luther King Jr. was an activist, an organizer, and an educator, a freedom fighter to the end. He was always evolving, and he was guided by a central dialectic: change is both inner and outer, spiritual and material, personal and social. King took seriously Mohandas Gandhi's well-known injunction: "We must be the change we wish to see in the world," and that meant always linking consciousness to conduct: "We all have a task and let us do it with a sense of divine dissatisfaction. Let us be divinely dissatisfied as long as we have a wealth of creeds and a poverty of deeds."

When King came out against the American war in Vietnam he enraged the Johnson administration and alienated much of his liberal support. But he held fast to the cause of humanity, against narrow notions of chauvinism and patriotism: "Every nation must now develop an overriding loyalty to mankind as a whole in order to preserve the best in their individual societies."

King's opposition to the war was consistent with his values and his ministry: his mission was nothing less than "to save the soul of America." King argued that the war was a "symptom of a much deeper malady within the American spirit," and that if we failed to address the deeper problem, "we will be marching and attending rallies without end": "I am convinced that if we are to get on the right side of the world revolution, we as a nation must undergo a radical revolution of values." He saw a radical revolution in values forcing us to look at the harsh reality of America in the world, and to reject whatever is unjust—"the glaring contrast of poverty and wealth," "the Western arrogance of feeling that it has everything to teach others and nothing to learn from them," the conquest and exploitation of other countries. "These are revolutionary times," he argued, times of upheaval against old systems of exploitation and oppression. Our task and our hope lie "in our ability to recapture the revolutionary spirit and go out into a sometimes hostile world declaring eternal hostility to poverty, racism, and militarism." If we fail to act, he said, we will be "dragged down the long, dark shameful corridors of time reserved for those who possess power without compassion, might without morality, and strength without sight." We need to teach toward freedom as a way to fight for a new world.

The American war in Vietnam and the black freedom struggle were entwined, connected, and not just in time, but in the issues each raised and in the sharp challenges each presented. The language of freedom was on our lips, the possibility of social change in the air. Each was about justice and simple fairness, each battered the myth of American innocence. Together they coalesced a set of standards we teachers might still aspire to: against conquest and persecution (whatever modern forms it might take), against cruelty and oppression, exploitation and extermination, for the universal rights of every human being. I was coming awake and it horrified me to realize that my government's protestations notwithstanding, the United States was a main perpetrator of pain and suffering in the wider world.

But looking backward settles nothing for today. What are the challenges to humanity today? What does the hope for democracy demand now? We are faced with the enduring stain of racism and the ever more elusive and intractable barriers to racial justice, the rapidly widening gulf between rich and poor, and the enthronement of greed. We are faced as well with aggressive economic and military adventures abroad, the macho posturing of men bonding in groups and enacting a kind of the-atrical but no less real militarism, the violence of conquest from Palestine to Puerto Rico to the Philippines.

The problems are huge, as always, and our ability to respond certainly seems puny by comparison. But respond we will, we must. As Jean-Jacques Rousseau said: You may not be interested in politics, but politics is interested in you. Teaching toward freedom is on the agenda.

Rousseau argues in regard to justice, equality "must not be understood to mean that degrees of power and wealth should be exactly the same," but only that with respect to power, equal-ity renders it "incapable of all violence" and only exerted in the interest of a freely developed and participatory law, and that with respect to wealth, "no citizen should be so opulent that he can buy another, and none so poor that he is constrained to sell himself." The quest for social justice over many centuries can be thought of as working within the open spaces of that ideal. Human beings suffer, of course, and they struggle, constructing and contesting all kinds of potential meanings of that dream, but nothing is settled once and for all.

For every human being life is, in part, an experience of pain and loss—there is always a tragic dimension to our brief life-times. But our living experience also embraces other ines-capable facts: we are all in this together, all passengers and crew on the same global spaceship, and too much (but not all) of what we suffer in life is the evil we visit upon one another; that is, it is unjustified suffering, unnatural loss, unnecessary pain—the kinds of things that ought to be avoidable, that we might even imagine eliminating altogether.

Encountering these facts thrusts us into the realm of human agency and choice, the battlefield of social action and change, where we come face to face with some stubborn questions: Can we, perhaps, stop the suffering? Can we alleviate at least some of the pain? Can we repair any of the loss? There are deeper con-siderations: Can society be changed at all? Is it remotely possible—not inevitable, certainly, perhaps not even likely—for people to come together freely, to imagine a more just and peaceful social order, to join hands and organize for something better, and to win?

If society cannot be changed under any circumstances, if there is nothing that can be done, not even small and humble gestures toward something better, well, that ends the conversation. Our sense of agency shrinks, our choices diminish, and our obligation to our fellow human beings ends. What more is there to say? It is sufficient then to simply wander weeping in the streets or to retreat into narcissism, concluding that human life is nothing more than a brutish, vicious, swamp war and that if I am to be spared, many, many others will have to be sacrificed, and I will agree to look on with indifference, or with at most a superficial nod toward compassion.

But if a fairer, more sane and just social order is both desirable and possible, that is, if some of us can join one another to imagine and build a participatory movement for justice, a public space for the enactment of democratic dreams, our field opens slightly. There would still be much to be done, for nothing would be entirely settled. We would still need to find ways to stir ourselves and our students from passivity, cynicism, and despair, to reach beyond the superficial barriers that wall us off from one another, to resist the flattening social evils like institutionalized racism, to shake off the anesthetizing impact of the authoritative, official voices that dominate so much of our space, to release our imaginations and act on behalf of what the known demands, linking our conduct firmly to our consciousness. We would be moving, then, without guarantees, but with purpose and with some small spark of hope. We would be teaching toward freedom.

The lifeblood of democracy here and throughout the world requires us to embrace differences and variety as strengths and not weaknesses. Democracy is animated by a kaleidoscope of backgrounds and capacities and abilities and hopes and dreams and aspirations. People must participate fully in all the decisions that affect their lives, speak with the possibility of being heard, listen with the possibility of being changed—democracy thrives on lateral, not vertical, channels of communication. These are the values that will animate democratic schools. Imagination is central to the democratic project, and cultivating the ability to see things as if they could be otherwise may be the centerpiece of a democratic education. Democratic values are grounded in the understanding that we are all in the same boat—it is silly to feel safe on the upper deck if great gashes are surging with water just below.

In the face of catastrophe, precisely when the broadest debate is needed, dissent is squashed. Politicians make predictable pronouncements, missiles are launched and bombs dropped. Teachers are subdued. The absence of any substantive resistance, of an organized political opposition, leaves a gaping void. Those of us who object, who refuse to get in line, are reduced to the role of dissidents. We are not a real presence, not yet, although these times cry urgently for debates and demonstrations, for meetings and protests, for generous and serious participation. We need to engage our fellow citizens, learn everything we can, participate in dialogues across backgrounds and experience. This is a shimmering pedagogic moment.

And what happens if we continue to display a few democratic forms and procedures, but simultaneously we destroy, or abandon, the *soul of democracy*? What if we lose the ability or the willingness of people to be fully engaged with others in a public sphere? What if our schools and our classrooms fail to promote and provoke democratic life? Without an awakened public, without an engaged citizenry, doesn't democracy become an empty shell?

Those of us who refuse to accede to the United States' attempt to dampen a republic of many voices need to link up with people the world over who are searching for a new way, who are resisting the powerful drive for profit above everything and the culture of selfishness and greed. We need to embrace a new kind of education, a different globalization, the models of which are everywhere—international scientific cooperation, cross-national environmental and feminist movements, international law and human rights campaigns. We need to build a global citizen resistance to war and empire, a movement for peace and balance.

In *The Cure at Troy* (1991), Seamus Heaney's reinterpretation of Sophocles' *Philoctetes*, the story of an outcast hero on the island of Lemnos, Philoctetes cries out, "The past is bearable, The past's only a scar, but the future—" Philoctetes is nursing a festering foot, a wound that both fouls the atmosphere and keeps him in howling fits of pain. When his comrades can no longer stand it, they abandon him on the island. A decade later, realizing that they desperately need his invincible bow to win the Trojan War, the Greeks are forced to return to Lemnos in an attempt to reconcile with Philoctetes.

This is the dramatization of public and private morality, of the tension between personal integrity and political expediency. Philoctetes has been injured, and for a decade he has eaten himself up, feeding on his wound, honing his sense of self-righteous rage. Can he forgive? Can he join those who wronged him? Or is he, the victim of injustice, intent on holding onto his wound, nurturing the wrong, just as the perpetrators of the injustice are intent on justifying their deeds?

Memory deceives, disorients, denies. We hold on to something—our afflictions, our rationalizations, our polished sense of self—as justification and purpose. But it is all scar tissue after all, the pain is faded, the anguish gone, the ecstasy an echo of a sigh. Nostalgia for a ship that has already left the shore leaves us stranded. What looms ahead is more terrifying, more challenging, and ultimately more satisfying. Knowing—even at this late date—that there are things to do, worlds to embrace, and

mostly that we are what we are not yet, might encourage us to
lift our heads and put, once again, one foot in front of the other.

Toward the end the chorus sings the human condition:

> Human beings suffer,
> They torture one another,
> They get hurt and get hard.
> No poem or play or song
> Can fully right a wrong
> Inflicted and endured.
>
> The innocent in gaols
> Beat on their bars together.
> A hunger-striker's father
> Stands in the graveyard dumb.
> The police widow in veils
> Faints at the funeral home.
>
> History says, *Don't hope*
> *On this side of the grave.*
> But then, once in a lifetime
> The longed-for tidal wave
> Of justice can rise up,
> And hope and history rhyme.
>
> So hope for a great sea-change
> On the far side of revenge.
> Believe that a further shore
> Is reachable from here.
> Believe in miracles
>
> And cures and healing wells.

This is a hope that bends toward action, links desire with doing,
and ties consciousness to conduct. Teaching toward freedom
grows from this hope.

* * *

Humanistic education opposes fear, ignorance, and helplessness by strengthening knowledge and ability. It enables people to question, to wonder, and to look critically. It requires teachers who are thoughtful, caring, and connected deeply to those they teach. This enabling education can be both the process by which people discover and develop various capacities as they locate themselves historically, and the vehicle for moving forward and breaking through the immutable facts, tradition, and objects of life as we find them. Its singular value is that it is education for freedom.

"Swifter than a weaver's shuttle," Job laments, "my life is but a breath." Our responsibility is to stay wide awake and engaged. And to choose. We recognize and insist that the present moment—in spite of what we are told—is not a point of arrival, but rather is as dynamic, unfulfilled, contested, packed with energy, and in play as any moment ever was or ever will be. History is being made right now; what we do or don't do matters. We shake ourselves awake, we look around. We act.

Education, of course, lives an excruciating paradox precisely because of its association with and location in schools. Education is about opening doors, opening minds, opening possibilities. School is too often on a mission of sorting and punishing, grading and ranking and certifying. Education is unconditional—it asks nothing in return. School demands obedience and conformity as a precondition to attendance. Education is surprising and unruly and disorderly and free, while the first and fundamental law of school is to follow orders. Education frees the mind, while schooling bureaucratizes the brain. An educator unleashes the unpredictable, while too many schoolteachers start with an unhealthy obsession with classroom management and linear lesson plans.

Working in schools—where the fundamental truths and demands and possibilities of teaching at its best are too often obscured and diminished and opaque, and where the powerful ethical core of our efforts can be systematically defaced and erased—requires a reengagement with the larger purposes of teaching. When the drumbeat of our daily lives is all about controlling the crowd, managing and moving the mob, conveying disembodied bits of information to inert things propped at desks before us, the need to fight for ourselves and our students becomes an imperative. Central to that fight is the understanding that there is no basis for education in a democracy except for faith in freedom and the enduring capacity for growth in ordinary people.

Teaching toward freedom goes beyond presenting what already is; it is teaching toward what could be, what ought to be, what is not yet. It is more than moral structures and guidelines; it includes an exposure to and understanding of material realities—advantages and disadvantages, privileges and oppressions—as well. Teaching of this kind might stir people to come together as vivid, thoughtful, and yes, outraged. Students, then, might find themselves dissatisfied with what had only yesterday seemed the natural order of things. At this point, when consciousness links to conduct and upheaval is in the air, teaching becomes a call to freedom.

There is an essential step teachers take in order to achieve a deeper connectedness to humanity—a step outside the safety of "home" into a wider world called "exile." Home is what is known, assumed, and safe, and those can be useful and positive things. But there comes a point when the known becomes dogma, the assumed becomes orthodoxy, and safety paranoia. It's time, then, to move on, and move out.

Bertolt Brecht said, "The exile's trade is hoping." The direction of exile is possibility, but something is lost, too—the anchor, the calm, the safe harbor. James Baldwin wrote of his years in Paris that he had been raised to believe in easy answers, and had gone to France in order to "put down all formulas and all safety in favor of the chilling unpredictability of experience." Should he have stayed at home? He couldn't, he asserts. "I think exile saved my life," Baldwin writes, "for it inexorably confirmed something which Americans have great difficulty accepting...: a man is not a man until he is able and willing to accept his own vision of the world."

We live in an age of forced migration and displacement, of exile and movement. In a sense all life is exile. But to choose exile is to consciously reach beyond, to become a wanderer, a hybrid with new awarenesses and allegiances. Nationalism is narrowing, patriotism coercive, tribalism a kind of violence to the soul. Dropping out can open a path to finding yourself as you discover a home in the wider world. This is not necessarily escapism, but might become a powerful new realism. Victor Hugo described exile as "not a material thing" but a "moral thing": "Any place one can daydream is good, provided the corner is dark and the horizon vast."

I want to think of myself as an exile, a refugee, and an expatriate by choice. I want to think of teachers as wanderers and seekers, not masters and commanders. This might allow us greater freedom to see the world through different and often surprising lenses, to make ourselves up as we go along, to rethink the orthodoxy of home, to experience our villages and states and nations as foreign countries, to jettison stereotypes, to wander with ourselves through an enlarged world, to develop a "double perspective," to learn different idioms, to transgress borders, to be mobile and playful, critical and accepting. And I am not alone. I send an invitation to my students; Let's go! Destination: Exile.

Teaching toward freedom begins with embracing what Liz Kirby, a young Chicago high school teacher, posits as a radically new three R's: Respect, Relevance, and Revolution. Reading, writing, and arithmetic still matter, of course, but the new three R's take us deeper—each is undertaken *based* on respect for students, *powered* by relevance and connectedness to their lived lives, *moving* toward revolution, transformation, change for them and for their world.

Respect. Freedom teachers are committed to the full visibility of persons, to their self-determined, self-actualized wholeness. We see our students as three-dimensional creatures, each unique, each sacred and unduplicable, each a distinct member of a larger society—we note the eternal dance of oneness and separateness that characterizes the human condition. We respect communities and families. We oppose anything that reduces them, that silences them or renders them opaque, anything that fragments or boxes or contains their humanity. We take their side in their quest for enlightenment and emancipation.

Relevance. Through dialogue, freedom teachers link student experiences and daily lives with deeper and wider ways of knowing, connect students with the world, opening our eyes to the concentric circles of context—social, historical, cultural, economic, spiritual—in which life is lived. Learning engages the five senses with the mind, joins heart and hand and brain. Henry Miller said, "The aim of life is to live, and to live means to be aware, joyously, drunkenly, serenely, divinely aware." We aim for awareness, conscious that there is always more to know and more to do.

Revolution. Freedom teachers recognize the unique capacity of human beings to self-consciously transform themselves as they act upon and change the world. We encourage our students to name the world, to identify obstacles, to join with others, to link their consciousness to their conduct, and to act. We nourish a social imagination, the capacity to look at the world as if it could be otherwise, as well as a spirit of activism combined with skepticism, urgency, and patience. We act, we doubt. The time is late and we have a long, long way to go.

What we hope for is a sense that injustice can be opposed and justice sought, a sense of ongoing unease, a spirit of connectedness and solidarity, of outrage tempered by generosity, and an open-ended dialogue that will never reach the last word.

We must think of ourselves less as determined and more as self-determining, less as categories, more as works in progress with an infinite array of unrealized capacities. We have a free will, we are free to open our eyes, free to name the world, free to make choices as citizens, not consumers. We are free to become the change we want to see, to become the people we've been waiting for.

We must remind ourselves what can power our hopes and our dreams. When I asked Studs Terkel how, at ninety years old, he was still the most energetic and hopeful person in the room, he began quoting e. e. cummings: "Don't let the bastards grind you down!" He continued, "Look at all I've seen through the years: I've seen people coming together, standing up, creating something out of nothing—unimaginable changes. A new world is needed, and we're the ones who can make it happen."

Toward the end of his life Myles Horton said something similar: "I've seen astonishing transformations. Think of the power of ordinary people in the South taking history into their hands and accomplishing extraordinary things." He went on to note that he lived in the Smokey Mountains, and sometimes walking at night he looked up at the massive Milky Way, realizing suddenly that "we're just a little speck of dust in the corner of an insignificant galaxy." "It's that combination," he said, "of awesome potential power and the fear of nothingness that gets me going every day."

At eighty-eight years old the revolutionary thinker and activist Grace Lee Boggs said, "People despair, when they presume they know what will happen. I'm hopeful because I know that the future, positive, negative or both, is unknowable. People who live hopefully do so because it's a more joyful, powerful way to live. We never know what impact our actions or words may have. So we act."

And the dazzling playwright Tony Kushner remarked on being blessed with "remarkable comrades and collaborators" with whom, he said, "we organize the world for ourselves, or at least we organize our understanding of the world—we reflect it, refract it, grieve over its savagery and help one another to discern amidst the gathering darkness, paths of resistance, pockets of peace, and places from whence hope may be plausibly expected."

Education ignites new ways of seeing the world, and so the fundamental message of the teacher begins with the belief that you can change your life. As this evolves, a necessary corollary emerges: transformed, you must change the world.

In Pablo Neruda's "The Poet's Obligation" (in *The Poetry of Pablo Neruda*, edited by Ilan Stavans, 2003), Neruda offered this advice to his fellow poets:

> To whoever is not listening to the sea
> this Friday morning, to whoever is cooped up
> in house or office, factory or woman
> or street or mine or dry prison cell,
> to him I come and without speaking or looking
> I arrive and open the door of his prison,
> and a vibration starts up, vague and insistent,
> a long rumble of thunder adds itself
> to the weight of the planet and the foam,
> the groaning rivers of the ocean rise,
> the star vibrates quickly in its corona
> and the sea beats, dies, and goes on beating.
>
> So, drawn on by my destiny,
> I ceaselessly must listen to and keep
> the sea's lamenting in my consciousness,
> I must feel the crash of the hard water
> and gather it up in a perpetual cup
> so that, wherever those in prison may be,
> wherever they suffer the sentence of the autumn,
> I may be present with an errant wave,
> I move in and out of windows,
> and hearing me, eyes may lift themselves,

asking "How can I reach the sea?"
And I will pass to them, saying nothing,
the starry echoes of the wave,
a breaking up of foam and quicksand,
a rustling of salt withdrawing itself,
the gray cry of sea birds on the coast.

So, through me, freedom and the sea
will call in answer to the shrouded heart.

If we understand the dry prison cell to be ignorance, cynicism, hopelessness, and all the entanglements of mystification and easy belief, and if we consider the sea's lamenting and the errant wave to represent a wider world and the hope for a brighter future, a time of greater human liberation, then we recognize this as the teacher's obligation as well, and further, the activist's obligation, the obligation of every purposeful life. We see the world in its fullness, the good and the bad of it. We feel its weight, we glimpse the many possible roads ahead. We must act, for we cannot pretend to be neutral on a moving train. But our actions should be tempered with doubt, with the knowledge that we've not got it completely right. We struggle to be wide awake to a dynamic, complex, and perspectival world. We work to improve life on the ground: right here, right now, in the particulars of daily life, with our colleagues and our students, with our expanding sense of community inside and outside of classrooms. We transform ourselves; we change the world. And, just like that, we are teaching toward freedom.

Acknowledgments

This book grew out of a series of public lectures I gave as a visiting scholar at Lesley University in Cambridge, Massachusetts, during the period August to December 2003. In 2002 I had given the June Fox Lecture, an annual event named for an emeritus professor and beloved longtime leader of the Lesley faculty. I met June, as well as several of her colleagues, on that first visit, and instantly experienced a kind of homecoming. This may seem odd, given that we were meeting for the very first time, and yet June felt like family to me, someone I had known forever, and the others were like old friends. Here was a community I recognized: progressive, forward leaning, dedicated to the ideals of democratic education and a just society. We more or less fell into one another's arms.

Some months later Caroline Heller, a remarkable colleague and glorious presence for several years at the University of Illinois at Chicago and now a professor at Lesley, and Anne Larkin, the energetic senior member of the faculty, contacted me about the possibility of returning to Lesley as a visiting scholar, teaching a research seminar and offering a series of public talks that might amplify the themes of the June Fox Lecture. I saw this generous invitation as an opportunity to work out some ideas in more detail, as well as a chance to collaborate with this formidable group of educators.

My time at Lesley was all that I had hoped it would be and more. Each visit was a moment of nourishment and challenge, each became a powerful, focused time for reenergizing, respiriting, and rethinking with people who live their teaching lives with acute purpose. This book is one result of that encounter.

I am indebted first and foremost to Caroline Heller for her generosity, her wisdom, her courage and integrity—and for getting the whole thing started. Without her support and help there would be no book. As Wilbur the pig says of the title character in *Charlotte's Web*, "It isn't often you meet someone who's both a good writer and a good friend." Caroline Heller is both.

Thanks to Anne Larkin, my steady host and guide, my coffee mate and consistent, thoughtful conversationalist. And thanks to her—and now my—good friend and colleague José Ribiero, who was a sparkling presence at the lectures, sharing his countrymen José Saramago and António Lobo Antunes with me and pointing out proper Portuguese pronunciation as necessary. José introduced me to the restaurant Atasca and Boston's vibrant Portuguese community as well.

Thanks to the faculty and staff at Lesley, especially Sandras Barnes, Marsha Bromfield, Paul Crowley, Arlene Dallalfar, William Dandridge, Frank Davis, Maura Delaney, Gene Diaz, Renny Harrigan, George Hein, Roberta Jackson, Sondra Langer, President Margaret McKenna, Provost Martha McKenna, Mary Mindess, Sarah Nieves-Squires, Judith Periale, Anne Pluto, Beverly Smith, William Stokes, and Carol Zigler.

And deep thanks to the graduate students I was privileged to work with, and who animated every visit: Helen Rasmussen, Ann Moritz, Kathy Nollet, Mary Sterling, Carol Watson-Phillips, Pebble Brooks.

I am grateful to the students and teachers I spoke with at the following institutions while working on this book, many of whom offered helpful insights: the Ann Arbor Open School, Antioch College, Humboldt State University, Lewis and Clark University, Loyola University, National Louis University, Northern Illinois University, Purdue University, University of South Carolina, Wesleyan College.

Rick Ayers, Greg Michie, and Amy Rome are three energetic, thoughtful, and compassionate teachers who helped me think and talk through the ideas presented in this book.

I am ever grateful to the smart, hardworking, and caring folks at Beacon Press, beginning with my peerless editor, Helene Atwan, who gives special meaning to the term "tough love." Whenever she cuts a word, a page, an entire chapter—which is often—and I complain that some day I'll publish those excised bits in my mythical "better book," she holds fast to her wiser judgments.

I wrote my first book on teaching fifteen years ago, and dedicated it "to my most persistent teachers," my children Zayd, Malik, and Chesa. Each is now grown up, each has edited—often informally, sometimes formally—subsequent books, and each continues to enlarge my experiences, to teach me about the world and its wonders. As our family grows—Rachel first, and then Magic—the lessons multiply. Eternal thanks. Malik also teaches high school now, and hanging out in his classroom inspired me while writing this work and added new dimensions to my understanding of what it means to be an engaged, caring, and thoughtful teacher.

Thanks to Paige James, a smart and careful reader, incisive editor, and freethinker. And thanks to my assistant, Diana Ruiz, whose skill and determined hard work and intelligence continue to be awesome.

As always, profound and ecstatic thanks to Bernardine Dohrn—we've shared a voyage together for thirty-five years, a mere blink of an eye it now seems.

Caroline Heller once told me about an interview she had heard with the Chicago playwright David Mamet, in which he said that there is only a fleeting moment when he considers himself a real writer: "You're only a writer *as* you write the last line," he said. "Before the last line," he continued, "you're a failed writer, and after the last line, you're an ex-writer." Thank you, again, from a failed ex-writer, still struggling to teach, still trying to make sense of the whole dizzying journey.

Credits